Interviewing for Journalists

Interviewing for Journalists details the central journalistic skill of how to ask the right question in the right way. It is a practical and concise guide for all print journalists – professionals, students and trainees – whether writing news stories or features for newspapers or magazines.

Interviewing for Journalists focuses on the many types of interviewing, from the vox pop and press conference to the interview used as the basis of an in-depth profile. Featuring interviews with a number of successful journalists such as Lynda Lee-Potter of the *Daily Mail* and Andrew Duncan of *Radio Times*, *Interviewing for Journalists* covers every stage of interviews including research, planning and preparation, structuring questions, the vital importance of body language, how to get a vivid quote, checking and editing material.

Interviewing for Journalists includes:

- Discussion of the importance of the interview for journalism
- Advice on how to handle different interviewees such as politicians, celebrities and vulnerable people
- How to carry out the telephone interview
- Hints on note-taking and recording methods, including shorthand
- Discussion of ethical, legal and professional issues such as libel, privacy, cheque-book journalism, off-the-record briefings and the limits of editing
- A glossary of journalistic terms and notes on further reading.

Sally Adams is a freelance journalist, editor and visiting tutor in journalism at the London College of Printing. She wrote the feature section of *Writing for Journalists*. **Wynford Hicks** is a freelance journalist and editorial trainer. He is the author of *English for Journalists*, now in its second edition, and *Writing for Journalists*.

Media Skills

Series Editor: Richard Keeble, City University, London
Series Advisers: Wynford Hicks and Jenny McKay

The *Media Skills* series provides a concise and thorough introduction to a rapidly changing media landscape. Each book is written by media and journalism lecturers or experienced professionals and is a key resource for a particular industry. Offering helpful advice and information and using practical examples from print, broadcast and digital media, as well as discussing ethical and regulatory issues, *Media Skills* books are essential guides for students and media professionals.

Also in this series:

English for Journalists 2nd edition
Wynford Hicks

Writing for Journalists
Wynford Hicks with Sally Adams and Harriett Gilbert

Interviewing for Radio
Jim Beaman

Producing for the Web
Jason Whittaker

Ethics for Journalists
Richard Keeble

Scriptwriting for the Screen
Charlie Moritz

Researching for Radio and Television
Adèle Emm

Reporting for Journalists
Chris Frost

Find more details of current *Media Skills* books and forthcoming titles at
www.producing.routledge.com

Interviewing for Journalists

Sally Adams

with an introduction and additional
material by Wynford Hicks

London and New York

First published 2001
by Routledge
11 New Fetter Lane, London EC4P 4EE

Simultaneously published in the USA and Canada
by Routledge
29 West 35th Street, New York, NY 10001

Routledge is an imprint of the Taylor & Francis Group

Typeset in Goudy Oldstyle
by Florence Production Ltd, Stoodleigh, Devon
Printed and bound in Great Britain
by MPG Books Ltd, Bodmin

British Library Cataloguing in Publication Data
A catalogue record for this book is available from the British Library

Library of Congress Cataloging in Publication Data
Adams, Sally, 1933–
    Interviewing for journalists/Sally Adams, with an introduction and
    additional material by Wynford Hicks.
        p. cm. – (Media skills)
    Includes bibliographical references and index.
    1. Interviewing in journalism.   I. Hicks, Wynford, 1942–   II. Series.
    PN4784.I6 A33 2001
    070.4'3–dc21   00–068416

ISBN 0–415–22913–8 (hbk)
ISBN 0–415–22914–6 (pbk)

Contents

Notes on authors

Sally Adams is a writer, editor and lecturer. She has worked as deputy editor of *She*, editor of *Mother and Baby* and *Weight Watchers Magazine*, as a reporter on the *Christchurch Press*, New Zealand, and as the letters page editor on the *San Francisco Chronicle*. She has written for the *Guardian, Daily Mail, Company, Evening Standard* and *Good Housekeeping*. She is a visiting tutor at the London College of Printing.

Wynford Hicks is a freelance journalist and editorial trainer. He has worked as a reporter, sub-editor, feature writer, editor and editorial consultant for newspapers, books and magazines and as a teacher of journalism specialising in sub-editing, writing styles and the use of English. He is the author of *English for Journalists*, now in its second edition, and *Writing for Journalists*.

1

Introduction

Wynford Hicks

Interviewing is the central activity in modern journalism. It is now the main means by which reporters and feature writers gather their material.

According to Christopher Silvester,[1] the interview came to Britain from the United States towards the end of the 19th century. It was part of the 'new journalism' that turned the media world upside down. From a stuffy, pompous thing that could interest only a minority of the serious-minded, journalism became a lively means of informing and entertaining millions of people.

As 20th-century journalism developed, interviewing became increasingly important. The journalist as observer and recorder, attending a political meeting to report the leader's speech in detail or describing shell-by-shell daily life in a town under fire or joining the mourners at a gangster's funeral, does still exist. But the journalist as interviewer now produces far more copy.

Even in sport the match report is followed by the post-match interview – and that's once a week. On the other six days the interview – with the sports star, the star's manager, the star's partner or one-night stand, the star's hairdresser – dominates. And let's not forget the sport star's 'column', based on an interview by a journalist on the sports desk.

In every area of newspaper and magazine coverage the interview is a way of bringing human interest into stories. It helps satisfy that powerful curiosity about the lives of the famous. But, much more than that, it is the means by which the journalist goes about gathering material. Interviews with experts and prominent people add credibility and authority to copy. Interviews with those involved in a news event – an eye-witness to an accident or a surviving victim – take a story beyond the reporter's necessarily restricted view.

In the Anglo-American tradition, interviewing sources and attributing facts and opinions to them is an essential part of reporting. Indeed, in many newspapers, otherwise sound stories that cannot be 'stood up' by supporting quotes remain unpublished.

And interviews can make news. A person who has publishable information can use an interview to reveal it at a time of their own choosing, perhaps promising the journalist an exclusive to try to ensure the kind of exposure they want. Or an enterprising reporter can track down a person they know or suspect has important information. The resulting interview then becomes the story.

The interview can be defined as a prearranged face-to-face meeting of a journalist, who asks questions, and an interviewee, who answers them. The interviewee is often notable (or notorious) and the questions usually focus on them, their life and opinions. But in this book we also use the wider definition that applies to all journalists who write news or features. Here interviewing is asking people questions to gather material for publication, both information and quotes.

So an interview may consist of a quick phone call to check a fact or an afternoon spent taping someone's life story. But brief or elaborate, a phone call or a face-to-face meeting, the successful interview comes from a professional approach. And it is the purpose of this book to explain and illustrate that approach, giving practical advice.

The book is based on the author's experience gained in many years of interviewing for a variety of newspapers and magazines and on a series of interviews with other journalists conducted for the book. Some of these – Lynda Lee-Potter, say, and Andrew Duncan – are well known; others less so; others again have chosen not to be named.

One consequence of asking practitioners how they work (as opposed to pontificating from the outside) is that there are occasionally differences of emphasis in their replies. More noticeable, though, is how much agreement there is on the essentials of interviewing: prepare thoroughly, listen carefully, edit accurately, and so on.

Interviewing for Journalists concentrates on print. But even here it is impossible to ignore the influence of broadcasting. For example, everybody in Britain has heard John Humphrys and seen Jeremy Paxman in action, so they're familiar with the confrontational interview. On the positive side interviewees now expect tough questioning when this is appropriate. But on the negative side trainee print journalists may be tempted to copy the Humphrys–Paxman approach – and needlessly antagonise their interviewees.

It's worth stressing that the tough broadcast interview is not a good model for the print journalist, particularly the beginner. By contrast, other broadcasters, such as Sue Lawley of *Desert Island Discs* or Anthony Clare of *In the Psychiatrist's Chair*, show what can be achieved by the softly-softly approach.

Another powerful influence on the print interview is the tape recorder – nowadays almost everybody is prepared to be taped. Tape makes a verbatim record possible and also enables the interviewer to concentrate on what the interviewee is actually saying, keeping eye contact. But on the downside transcription takes a long time and the printed interview, if not well edited, can be wordy and repetitive.

It's a truism that this is a media-conscious age: academic media studies courses abound and there is some (though not enough) practical journalism training. And just as some journalism students and trainee journalists practise interviewing, their counterparts go on media-awareness courses and practise being interviewed.

Politicians and business people have been organising coaching for themselves for years but now everybody's at it. Even the 3,500 judges in England and Wales get a booklet (*The Media, a Guide for Judges*) telling them how to handle interviews without getting rattled and how to react if they're doorstepped by a posse of hacks.

If anything confirms the need for good, thorough journalism training, it's the inclusion of interview techniques and news management skills in corporate training schemes. As one ex-journalist who trains executives puts it in Chapter 5, 'There are whole chunks of journalism effectively run by PR companies.'

The core of this book is the prearranged set-piece interview, which we take you through in stages from research and planning to checking and editing quotes. (Writing as such is not covered in this book but in another in the series: *Writing for Journalists*.)

We start with a chapter on routine interviewing which provides some basic advice for trainees on, for example, how to follow up a press release or a reader's tip.

We cover telephone interviewing and note-taking and recording in separate chapters and also discuss approaches to different kinds of interviewees – politicians, celebrities and some special cases: reluctant and inexperienced interviewees; vulnerable people, children and the bereaved; the PR sitting in on the interview and interviewers doubling up.

This section does not claim to be 'comprehensive'. For example, although we refer to the investigative journalist at points during the book, we have not attempted to give advice on how to work undercover, how to lay traps for corrupt politicians, etc.

Nor have we covered the so-called questionnaire interview which consists of supplying a list of standard questions usually by fax, then editing the answers.

By all means do it if your editor asks you to (or as a fallback, second-best to a phone interview) but don't call it interviewing.

In the book various issues – ethical, legal, professional – raised by the practice of interviewing are discussed as they arise. These points are brought together in the final chapter. This chapter has been particularly hard to write. It is one thing to lay down general principles and draft codes of practice – especially for other people to follow. It is much harder to decide what to do in specific situations. So if there is a lack of certainty in some of the advice offered it is because, ultimately, you the journalist must find your own answers to the questions raised.

Note

1   C. Silvester, *The Penguin Book of Interviews: An Anthology from 1859 to the Present Day*, Viking, 1993.

2
Basics

Skilled journalists make interviewing look easy. They quickly get on their interviewee's wavelength and encourage them to talk freely. They ask questions that elicit lively replies, listen to what's said, note what they hear while thinking of the next question, at the same time checking what they've just heard against what they know from research.

They cajole answers from the reluctant, corral the waffly, reassure the nervous, recognise fudges, check ambiguities – and all within a set time with someone they've probably never met before. They make it look easy but it isn't. If journalism is a craft, interviewing is an art. There are a lot of unrelated skills to master and, like learning to drive a car, interviewing is daunting and difficult at first. But with practice, setting off smoothly, signalling, changing gear, steering and watching the instruments become second nature. So it is with interviewing.

The most useful characteristic for an all-round interviewer is to be likeable, the sort of person who can get on with almost anybody and is interested in everybody: a person who people are happy to talk to, who comes across as a human being first, a journalist second.

The most valuable attribute is probably curiosity, followed by charm, keen powers of observation, doggedness, flexibility and fairness. Then add the ability to think fast, analyse, keep a poker face when necessary, a broad general knowledge and plenty of scepticism . . .

It's a rare journalist who can master the complete range of styles interviewing demands. An interviewer who's a brilliant fact-extractor is unlikely to produce a good interview with an unhappy transsexual for *Marie Claire*, just as a sympathetic and understanding feature specialist probably wouldn't produce a good interview with the chancellor of the exchequer for *Investors Chronicle*. Each type of interview requires a different approach. Then, to add to the complications, there are the abrasions of personality to consider. This is why self-effacing interviewers can be so successful, like the 'invisible' photographer who people forget is there.

Interviewing is also a skill best mastered progressively. There's a certain order to it as there is in life. Just as children crawl before they walk, walk before they run and run before they play football – so it is with interviewing and, comfortingly, it's something you get better at with age.

If you want to become a good all-round interviewer – the equivalent of a skilled footballer – please start here with routine interviews. Skipping the basics is the equivalent of hitting the ground running with zero practice.

First, it's important to realise what the interviewer/interviewee relationship entails. You will use people and you will be used. You will find some people who divulge little, others who tell you more than you wish to know. You will be trusted with secrets, you will be lied to. You will be bombarded with what seem like irrelevancies and only later realise what a key piece one of them is in the information jigsaw. You will be rebuffed, you will be courted.

As a result of what you write, based on what you learn during an interview, people may lose their jobs, companies may close, lives may be ruined. Or you may be intrigued enough to try out a new sport, meet someone you later marry, win an award.

Some interviewees will later ask you to pretty up or sanitise their words. Some may beg you not to print what they said, some may threaten. These decisions usually rest with the editor but a time may come when you are the one who has to decide. Journalists who have been interviewed and regret what they have said, or fear they will be misrepresented, will understand. A former *Mirror* writer involved in a shares scandal (Anil Bhoyrul, City Slicker columnist) said after he'd been sacked, 'I've written some pretty nasty things about people but when it's done to you it's bloody awful.' For most journalists, the first time someone pleads with them to alter copy is when the real power of the press hits home.

Editorial policy

Let's assume, first, that you are working for a publication that has an editorial policy, i.e., knows what it is trying to achieve and why. This should describe realistically how the publication intends to reach its readers – for example, by amusing or informing them, by helping or persuading them. Editorial policies are important because if you don't know what you are trying to achieve, you're flailing round in a fog.

Second, let's assume that you work for a publication that knows a lot about its readers and understands how to interest them. And third, that it's a publication where they send you out to get stories face-to-face as well as on the telephone. Here we're talking about an ideal, of course. All too often in newspaper and magazine offices the emphasis is on productivity and speed. Reporters now mostly interview over the phone and going out on a story can be seen as a luxury.

To learn the trade, trainee journalists need to get out of the office to meet people. Get it right face-to-face and you learn *all* the interviewing skills. Learn on the telephone and your repertoire will be incomplete.

Interviewing is the journalist's basic tool. You interview to get a story, quotes, background, opinion. You really can't do this until you have a good grasp of the six indispensable journalistic questions – *who?*, *what?*, *when?*, *where?*, *why?* and *how?* – and know why they are essential. You must also understand that there's not one single answer to each of them. *Who?* for a local paper may well be Sam Smith, 35, of Islip, Northants. *Who?* for a trade journal may well be J. Samuel Smith, managing director of Dragees International's London office. *Who?* for a magazine may well be Psychic Sam, the man who predicts your future.

Communication

One more necessity. We can't start until we have looked at the maze that is communication. When two people communicate, a lot can go wrong in a very short time. Say we call a (male) interviewer A and a (female) inter-viewee B. In a simple question and answer exchange you have to take into account the following:

> What A thinks he says.
> What A actually says.
> What B thinks she hears.
> What B actually hears.
> What B actually says in reply.
> What A thinks he hears B say.

A is interviewing B about arguments at work. B is talking about a row at a previous job.

> B ends by saying 'So I left.'
> B thinks she has said: 'I left work early that day.'
> A thinks he hears: 'So I quit my job.'
> A says: 'Did you regret the decision?'
> B thinks 'What a stupid question.'
> B says: 'No.'
> A thinks B is glad she left her previous job and is happy in her present one, which may or may not be true.

Or:

> A is interviewing B about experiences as an adult education teacher and
> asks, 'How do you get on with the old?'
> B hears real insensitivity, 'the old' not 'older people'. Starts to go off A
> immediately.
> B replies: 'Older people are exceptionally rewarding to teach.'
> A agrees enthusiastically: 'Yes, aren't they – the old have got so much
> to learn.' A thinks that sounds understanding.
> B sees it as showing that A thinks older people are stupid.

This applies at all levels. Alan Greenspan, chairman of the US government's
powerful Federal Reserve Bank, is on record as telling Wall Street economists:
'I know you believe you understand what you think I said but I am not sure
you realise that what you heard is not what I meant.'

The best way to avoid misunderstanding is to use feedback: if at all uncertain, repeat back to your interviewee what you believe they said. This doesn't
mean you paraphrase every word slowly and clearly, enunciating distinctly,
but that you recognise accuracy is in both your interests and there are many
factors which can cause mistakes. These include – for both of you – stress,
prejudice, tiredness, distraction, a closed mind.

Basic interviewing

Reduced to its essentials, interviewing couldn't be simpler:

- Ask clear questions
- Listen to the answers
- Encourage the interviewee to keep talking

This is the recommended way to start and master the essential journalistic
skills: working to a deadline, getting details right, approaching people confidently, recognising a good story when you see one, getting good quotes and
writing a simple, uncluttered intro.

BASIC PRINCIPLES

Before you interview anyone you must

- **Plan**. It's essential you know what you want to know, so go in with your
  questions or topics prepared.

It's also very important that you

- **Research**. Find out as much as you possibly can about your interviewee
  before you meet them. Sometimes this won't be possible but recognise

that being prepared is what gives you the edge and is essential in business and political interviews.

During the interview you should

- **Listen**. No talking journalist ever held a good interview – silence really is golden.
- **Empathise**. This doesn't mean you have to like your interviewee, but that you think yourself into their skin and work out the likely impact of your questions.

These four principles underpin all successful interviews. In addition you should:

- Always tell your interviewee who you are. Give your name and say who you're working for.
- Fit in. Dress in a way that suits your interviewee. Use language they feel comfortable with.
- Get all the basic details. For local papers the 'must-knows' are routinely name, age, occupation and address. Full and precise identification is essential. A father and son living at the same address may have the same name. Always check spellings, however obvious a name may appear. Ann with or without an e? Thompson with or without a p? Charlie or Charley? Ian or Iain?
- For specialist reporters and magazine writers, a person's age may be irrelevant so the 'must-knows' are different. For a business paper they probably include job title rather than occupation. For a slimming magazine a person's weight and height.
- Listen and record. Don't argue, judge, laugh or show embarrassment.
- Try to ask questions in a logical order. If your questions hop about in a weird way it confuses your interviewee.
- Recognise that quotes – and luck – count. Learn to ask good questions in a way that encourages good quotes. It's partly down to practice and partly luck. Some people are more quotable than others.
- Hold your ego in check.
- Think pix. Never forget the picture angle when you're working on a story.
- Be prepared to learn from your mistakes.

Always remember:

- The interviewee is the star.
- Be sceptical rather than adversarial.
- 'You get more flies with honey than vinegar.'

Calls

On a local paper doing the calls – phoning the police, fire and ambulance services regularly to check whether they have a story – is the simplest kind of interviewing. Your manner should be businesslike and courteous as you will have many calls to make. From most of these you'll get nothing worth passing on to the news editor, but every so often you'll learn of an incident that needs following up.

Vox pops

The term comes from the Latin *vox populi* meaning 'voice of the people'. Often an easy way to fill a page is with pix and short quotes from people interviewed on the street about current topics. Success depends on the topic chosen.

It may be valid to ask Manchester United fans their views about whether the manager should keep a player who wants to leave. But asking people on the street for their comments on decisions made by the General Medical Council, say, or the president of Russia in the face of a crisis, is unlikely to reveal much of value.

However, vox pops are a great way to practise basic interviewing skills on willing interviewees, who seem flattered to be asked – not always the reaction of people faced with beginners. Vox pops work because you learn to get basic details, precise answers and good quotes. Without ruining the story, you can discard any interviews that don't work either because the answers were uninteresting or because you got it wrong. You learn to ask the main question, listen to the answer and then seek extra value/mileage from supplementaries/follow-ups.

The way to approach a vox pop is, first, to ensure you have a relevant question likely to appeal to people in your area, then to walk up to people confidently, notebook in hand. Don't use a clipboard – that signals market research. Use the word 'journalist' as early as possible in your introduction. Smile, of course, and be positive.

If you are worried about approaching strangers, it's likely they'll refuse to talk to you. This is evidence of one of the great laws of interviewing, that of reciprocity: you get back what you send out.

> Message: 'I'm nervous, have never done this before and am certain no one will talk to me.'
> Response: 'Do I want to talk to this scared person? No, I don't.'

Message: 'You look interesting. I'd like to know what you think and so, I'm sure, would my readers.'
Response: 'Why not?'

The best way to find people likely to talk is to look for the journalistic equivalent of a captive audience: people who are already standing still, waiting for a bus, for instance, or in a queue to get into a club. Shopping centres and street markets can be productive areas. Use your common sense, though, and don't approach people with huge bags of shopping or, say, three small children who are playing up. Market traders who aren't serving people are usually good for a quote. The best prospects are those whose eye you catch, or you could select people you'd like to know better.

'Hi, I'm a journalist interviewing people about . . . and I'd just like a minute or two to discover what you think.'

'Hello, I'm a journalist and I'd be very grateful if you'd spare me some time to talk about . . .'

'Hello, I'm a journalist writing a feature on . . . It'll just take a minute . . .'

Give your name and the publication you're working for fairly early, but there's no need yet to take their name. Get them talking first. It's best to stand opposite your interviewee. This works because it actually impedes their movement, making any attempt to get away from you obvious.

Ring rounds

A variation on the vox pop can be done on the phone, but with a ring round you're calling specific people – e.g. retailers of Christmas trees – not approaching strangers at random. Again, if the odd one doesn't co-operate, you can drop them from your story.

To give the quotes authenticity it's important to preserve the words and speech patterns of the people interviewed – which means having good shorthand.

Press release follow-up

What divides worthwhile journalism from some of the less rewarding varieties being practised is often pointed up by attitudes to press releases. In worthwhile journalism, a press release is often the starting point for a story. What happens is that the journalist reads the release, then gets on the phone and starts asking questions.

At the very least, the journalist will want to angle the story to suit the readers and get some good quotes. But often what follows goes much further. Here's a press release.

RUN FOR THE TRUST IN THE LONDON MARATHON

Keen marathon runners are being invited to don their running shoes and run for The Prince's Trust in the Flora London Marathon taking place this year on Sunday, 13 April.

This year is a particularly special year for The Prince's Trust as it will be celebrating its 21st birthday. The Trust is therefore keen to encourage as many runners as possible to join their team to make it the biggest ever for the world's most popular marathon.

Anyone running for The Trust will receive a free running vest and the chance to win some excellent prizes including a Sony PlayStation. The team will also be invited to a post-Marathon celebratory reception yards from the finishing line, where they will be treated to well-earned food and refreshments; hot showers and massages will also be available.

The Trust welcomes runners who have already secured Marathon places but also has a number of places available for runners who have not been successful in the applications but wish to run and raise funds on The Trust's behalf.

If you're a reporter on the London *Evening Standard* what would you ask the Prince's Trust press officer? Here are a few ideas:

- There are no quotes in the press release. Would it be possible to speak to the Prince of Wales to get his personal comment on the idea? (Always aim for the top.)
- If not the Prince of Wales, is there anybody else who could speak on behalf of the Trust?
- Did the Prince's Trust do the same thing last year? If so, how many runners were there in the Trust's team? Anybody well-known, either as an athlete or a celebrity?
- How will this year's runners 'raise funds on the Trust's behalf'?
- Has anybody well-known agreed to take part so far?
- What's the target in terms of numbers of runners?
- What will the 'well-earned food and refreshments' be? Caviar and champagne or something less frivolous – organic wholemeal bread, raw carrot and fruit juice?
- What are Sony putting in besides a PlayStation and what are they getting out?

If there is a negative story to unearth – and in business there often is – some PRs believe they can hide it by boring journalists to death, so read the release carefully to find where the gaps are. A common spot to hide bad news is somewhere around pars six to eight.

Covering press conferences

The old bear-baiting scrums of the movies are dead. In these days of sophisticated, focused PR, press conferences are fewer and much more controlled. Best advice now: arrive early and ask the PR about the agenda.

Has the main speaker agreed to talk for 20 minutes, take questions for five and then dash away? Or will they be available for private questioning afterwards? If so, for how long? Is there going to be a group of favoured correspondents given private access? If so, can you muscle in on it?

The other thing to discover is what handouts are on offer and when. To avoid the grab-it-and-run syndrome, PRs rarely give out press releases at the check-in desk or before the event. However, even if detailed press releases are promised at the end of the conference, always make notes. First, because speakers may go off-script and it's then you'll get the liveliest quotes. Second, because PRs routinely leave statistics shown on screen or OHP *out* of handouts in self-protection. Companies may not want competitors to know how they value the opposition's market share.

Don't be afraid to ask simple questions. The speaker mentions KEGXL as a contributing factor to the company's success. You haven't a clue what it is. As a beginner, dare you ask? Journalists dislike appearing stupid in front of their peers and this is probably well founded in the first few weeks on a specialist publication, when asking a basic question can give everyone the impression you are a fool in the wrong job – but it's much more important not to appear stupid in print. So make you sure you find out what KEGXL is, somehow. Ask the PR later. They won't think you daft, but will be delighted that you're checking.

Try to sit near the front, so you won't miss what's going on and when you do ask a question, identify yourself exactly, as in all interviewing: 'Mark Brown, the *Nation*.'

Most journalists hate to ask their best questions in open forum at a press conference, allowing everyone to benefit from the answer when, with a little organisation, they can talk to the main speaker one-to-one and get an exclusive. So after the conference there's usually a queue of journalists waiting to talk to the speaker, hoping no one will overhear and steal a juicy quote. Sometimes journalists cluster round and the best plan then is to wait until everyone else, or at least your main competitor, has gone. Failing that, if deadlines allow, ask the speaker or PR for time alone with them.

What you should never do after a conference is take your eye off the speaker or they may be whisked away. If you're on a long deadline, you may be able to contact them later, but for immediate deadlines, stick close. No matter what promises speakers or PRs have made, in the competing pressures of a press conference things go awry. So keep the speaker in sight and, if you can, keep an eye on the PR too.

If the speaker is going to be whisked away and you have to ask your best question in public, there are two possibilities. First, wait until the conference is nearly over, most questioners are flagging and everyone's getting restive. Make your preamble wordy and hope most people will switch off and read back their notes instead of listening.

The other ploy for specialists in a conference filled with generalists with a watching brief in your subject is to ask your question in jargon. For instance, use initials that the speaker will understand but most of the audience won't.

Following up a tip

Dramatic event, sketchy details

The news desk of a busy twice-weekly paper gets a tip that there's a house on fire in one of the surrounding estates and the address is confirmed by a call to the fire service. You're delayed in traffic and get there to find a smouldering building; the fire brigade has left. You see an elderly neighbour in her front garden looking at the burnt remains. After introducing yourself do you start with

'What's the name of the people next door?' (*Who?*)

'Was anybody home next door when the fire started?' (*More Who?*)

'What time did the fire start?' (*When?*)

'Do you know why it started?' (*Why?*)

Well, not if you have any sense.

The key question to ask yourself for an interview such as this – a dramatic event where you have a very sketchy idea of the story – is 'Who knows more about the fire: you or the neighbour?' Obviously the neighbour does. So after a few sympathetic words, the most sensible thing to say is: 'Please tell me what happened.' Then listen and, at the end, go back and ask questions to fill in the gaps.

Let us suppose the neighbour takes a deep breath and says:

'It was terrible, absolutely terrible. That poor, poor girl. I was watching the telly when I heard the dog next door barking. It was frantic barking, most unlike him. So I went out into the back garden and saw smoke pouring out of the kitchen window. I knew Fran was at home and thought she might not know of the fire, so I hurried out the front but it was terrible, I could see a horrible orange glow in the hall.

'Just then I saw her – trying to open the upstairs bedroom window, screaming for help. I didn't know what to do. The heat was so fierce. At that moment, the fire brigade arrived, thank God, and they'd got their ladder up to the window within minutes and saved Fran. She's gone to the district hospital. Dennis will be home any minute ...' [Her voice trails away.]

At this point, you make more sympathetic noises about what a shock it must have been and how terrible for her and everyone and could she just confirm what happened? Start by checking how she spells her name. Then you start filling in gaps: Fran's full name, how she spells it and what she does; who Dennis is and what he does; what sort of dog it was and did he survive ... and so on.

Try not to succumb to what has been called 'the journalist's disease': being more certain about events than the people who were actually there. Later, of course, you would follow up with a phone call to the fire service and the hospital, hope to talk to Dennis and get a fuller story.

Unlike features, news stories have a lot in common. Reporters from different papers covering the same story are likely to produce similar stories. One may be sharper, brighter, than the other but they will be recognisably the same. Bill Browne, a former news editor of the Southampton *Evening Echo* says:

'My biggest mistake as a junior was to think the deadline was so important that you got in and got out as quickly as you could. Now I know the longer you stay, the better story you write. Milk every job for every last line you can get out of it then, when the news editor asks you a question about what you haven't included, you can answer it. Rush away if the deadline demands it, but don't rush away just because you think that's what journalists do.'

Time to research

The news desk of a busy weekly paper gets a call from a woman in an outlying village on the edge of town complaining that the signposts directing traffic to the village from the south have been removed after the introduction of a new junction. She's been in touch with the county council but they refuse to reinstate the signs. The news editor gives you the woman's address and tells you to check out the story.

This requires several interviews and a fair number of phone calls. There are multiple *whos?* – the woman, the county council surveyor or traffic planner, possibly other villagers, maybe confused motorists. You would need their basic details, e.g. name and how spelt, job title (for the officials), age and address (for the villagers – address for your records but not printed) and, if a motorist, where going, where from, how long the journey took, etc. In this example, details of the contact villager would include name and how spelt, how long she'd lived in the village and if she occupied any village position (clerk to the parish council, post mistress, or whatever).

For *what?* you have to check that the information is right and that the village signposts are not being replaced. Most news tips are inaccurate in some respect. Confirmation or denial will come from talking to the county council officer and driving to the junction.

For *where?* you need to establish the exact road involved and maybe its number, then how people coming from the south looking for the village are expected to get there, i.e., the new route. For *when?* you need to check exactly when the signs were taken away.

The *how?* answer seems to be closely linked to *why?*, which means checking with the county council surveyors/planning department in the county town. *Why?* is often the hardest and most rewarding question. In this instance it could be that the new junction has been installed to allow access to a new estate which is about to be developed, and national guidelines will not permit through traffic to be signed through residential estates.

This done, you make an appointment to see the villager who complained and get quotes from her and maybe two of her friends she's invited in to meet you, all expressing their fury at living in a Domesday village that appears to have been wiped off the map.

3
Preparing and getting started

Successful interviewing is based on preparedness – being ready for anything and everything that might happen. This is a state of mind that comes from confidence: confidence based firmly on forethought, planning and research.

Preparation

The recommended formula for feature interviews used to be 'an hour's preparation for every 10 minutes of interview time'. Few journalists now enjoy such luxury to plan their approach, but the advice contains a basic truth: thorough preparation is vital. 'Plan' is to interviewing what 'think' is to journalism: the basic activity that underpins all the rest. As Bill Browne, now editor of the Basingstoke *Gazette*, recounts:

> 'As a really wet-behind-the-ears junior, I was told at ten minutes' notice to go to a bookshop and interview a famous author. So famous that I didn't know what she'd done [sailed round the world single-handed]. I walked in with a general question like "Can you tell me about your interest in sailing?" and she said, "You obviously haven't done any research." There was a pause and she added, "Now he's trying to think of something sensible to ask me."
>
> The fault was mine. I could have stopped by the library on the way to the bookshop, taken five minutes to look at the clips. It was my first celebrity interview. The best lesson I could ever have had.'

Persist

Once you know who you wish to interview, you need to persuade them to talk to you. It helps to have a good reputation and to work for a highly rated publication. Even then, persistence is important.

Newly arrived from Australia, journalist Phillip Knightley freelanced for the *Sunday Times*. On one occasion, given a good lead, he failed to get the interview and received the following advice from a colleague which, he says, had a resounding effect on his career:

> 'Most people are modest or like to give that impression. So when you want to put them in the limelight they'll say no. But they don't mean it. They're waiting for you to ask again, so that they can surrender gracefully and modestly . . . In journalism, no "no" is ever final.'

What can you do if you're unknown and work on an unappealing title? First, step into your target's shoes and try to establish what will persuade them to drop their defences. It could be publicity, exposure, a raised profile; perhaps the opportunity to put their side of a story, to correct inaccuracies. You have to persuade them of your worth and substance, too.

If you're approaching a person, company or organisation with an agent or PR, you can phone or write, putting your request in a positive light. It took me a day to write the letter that got me on to a nuclear submarine. I dredged my background for details that would allay fears in the naval mind about freelance journalists.

Writing direct to the person works well. (For a superb example of a persuasive letter see Appendix 3.) Many addresses are in *Who's Who* and, working from cuttings, using a combination of the telephone directory, maybe the electoral register and post code guides, it's amazing what can be discovered. You can always use an intermediary to vouch for you or mention their name in a phone call or letter. Check with your referee first, of course.

Writing long term pays off, too. Phillip Knightley corresponded with the spy Kim Philby for over 20 years before getting an interview with him in Moscow just before he died. Politicians, gifted with a keen sense of priority, may put on hold interviews with publications they see as tangential to their immediate interests. It took two years of persistent reminders by Nick Pigott, editor of *Railway* magazine, before the then secretary of state for the environment, transport and the regions made good his promise of an exclusive interview.

Enterprise pays off

An aviation chief executive involved in a tremendous brouhaha and besieged by phone calls from the press ducked into the trenches and let his secretary take the calls, refusing every request for an interview. Over the course of a few days of fruitless phoning, his secretary got to know members of the press. Turning down Lynda Lee-Potter's nth request for an interview, she said her boss had just left the factory to catch a train to London for a meeting.

Lee-Potter knew where the factory was, consulted the timetable and met the train, waiting at the barrier. 'Mr . . .,' she said, recognising him from his photograph, 'I'm Lynda Lee-Potter of the *Daily Mail*. Could you spare me some time?' Deeply impressed, he agreed. Of such are scoops made.

Lynn Barber says she got her 'only real scoop', an interview with reclusive billionaire John Paul Getty, after falling for a hoax Getty. It became a sort of crusade to interview the real one. 'I kept writing to him every week and to his solicitor Vanni Treves, and eventually Mr Treves summoned me to his office, and I suppose he must have liked me, because soon afterwards he took me to interview Mr Getty.'

As a last resort, when a previously much-written-about person has gone to ground, you could try this. A powerful chief executive about to retire refused all requests for an interview from *Financial Times* journalist Ken Gooding. Gooding went through the file and picked out all the peculiarities ever written about the man but never denied: that he always walked to work but made his chauffeur follow him in the car; that he wore a pink rose in his button-hole on Mondays, a yellow one on Tuesdays . . .

> 'I picked out all the stupid bits and made him look the most bizarre person in the world, then sent the copy round. He was on the phone within five minutes. Of course, a more sophisticated person might have got his lawyer on the phone.'

Identify your targets – correctly

This sort of blunder happens very rarely, but when it does it's stamped permanently in the records. The *Observer* in July 2000 printed the novelist Roddy Doyle's selection of summer reading: *Wild Swans*, *Enduring Love* and *An Instance of the Fingerpost*. 'I think three books is plenty,' he was quoted as saying. Only one problem. This Roddy Doyle wasn't the Irish novelist, author of *The Commitments* and *Paddy Clarke, Ha Ha Ha*. He was a computer engineer from north London.

Roy Plomley, originator of *Desert Island Discs*, recounts how he took the best-selling novelist Alistair MacLean, author of *The Guns of Navarone*, out to lunch before the recording. They chatted easily though novels weren't mentioned. Finally Plomley asked 'Which part of the year do you put aside to do your writing?' 'Ah!' said his guest. 'I'm not Alistair MacLean the writer. No, I'm in charge of the European Tourist Bureau of the Government of Ontario.' Be warned.

Fixing appointments

Most appointments are made on the phone. As you can't see what your inter-viewee or their secretary/PA is doing, it's wise to be pernickety.

First, you need to identify yourself and your publication, give them an idea of what you want to talk to them about and a rough idea of how long it might take. It's important to phrase your request so that they sense how they'll benefit. A proper sense of urgency and pride in your publication helps.

Be especially careful when agreeing an appointment to check the date, month and day of the week. You may not be looking at the wrong month in your diary, but your interviewee may. So make it: 'That's Wednesday, 14 October at 3.30pm – right?'

Interviews over lunch go well, lubricated with alcohol, but you then need either a quiet restaurant and a good tape recorder with a directional mike or the ability to take notes while you eat one-handed, which limits what you order.

Few people now have the time to eat first and be interviewed afterwards. And anyway, if you appear at all interested in them, they're bound to say something quotable while eating, so you'd have to get out your notebook or tape recorder anyhow. Beware of crowded pubs, cafes, theatre lobbies, and anywhere with background music. Many people are more benevolent, chatty and relaxed after lunch so, if the interviewee or the subject is at all tricky, try for the afternoon. Your place or mine? No contest: theirs. They'll feel more at home and you can see the house, desk, factory, workshop, studio – and how they relate to the people there.

If necessary, establish how to get there. If the directions sound at all complicated, ask them to fax a map. Be very careful when taking down instructions. Never, ever, accept those that start 'Take the second on the right after you come under the bridge' for the obvious reason that (a) there may be more than one bridge; (b) you or your interviewee may not know from which direction you will approach the bridge. Bitter experience speaking. Ask for, and get, road names. This helps cut out the mistakes which occur when you're told 'take the third on the left' whereas it's really the fourth but your interviewee has never noticed one of the roads or doesn't rate it.

You may ask for about 40 minutes and the interviewee may say, 'Sorry – can spare you just 15.' Depending on their tone of voice, decide whether to ask for extra time and risk offending them, so getting off on the wrong foot, or accept what they offer and then ensure that the interview is really interesting. Unless you're dealing with a chief executive or someone on a fixed timetable or catching a plane, you're likely to be given the extra time.

Brian Hayes of *Radio Five Live* said he could spare one freelance a quarter of an hour. Forty-five minutes later they were still talking and, at the end, the freelance mentioned he'd been generous with his time. 'Just wanted to be able to get rid of you if necessary,' Hayes said.

Ditto a man who I was told was very sticky but would be OK after half an hour. 'I'll give you 30 minutes,' he said. So I boiled my questions down to condensed soup, but 90 minutes later we were still talking.

Lastly, when fixing appointments, be sure to make contingency plans: where they can reach you if they have to cancel; where they're likely to be if you have to cancel.

What to take with you

Ideally, stowed somewhere in or near your desk is a file, briefcase or folder that contains most of what you need. What's in the pack depends on the journalist and the publication. A suggested list follows. Before you leave, check everything's there and make any necessary last-minute additions.

- notebook of a suitable size (plus spare if notebook in use is nearly full) – small unobtrusive pocket notebooks are growing in popularity, rivalling the spiral ring-bound A5 reporter's notebook. Please don't use A4 pads;
- business cards;
- pens/pencils;
- tape digital recorder with the voice-activated control switched permanently off;
- ready to record tape in position, pre-identified with interviewee's name and date of interview;
- spare tapes;
- spare batteries;
- mobile phone/phone card;
- loose change for phone calls, parking meters, etc.;
- map;
- address and telephone number of person to be interviewed;
- directions to get there;
- copy of publication if appropriate;
- maybe folding umbrella/flatpack raincoat/paper handkerchiefs/passport/sunscreen . . .

What to wear

People talk most easily to those they perceive as being like themselves. Work from there. Politicians and most business people wear suits or at least fairly traditional clothes so it's a great mistake to arrive in shorts or jeans. One sober-suited chief executive said: 'A young journalist who arrives looking as though they've just walked out of a protest, wearing Hush Puppies and corduroy trousers, immediately fixes themselves in a subordinate position.'

The way interviewees dress shows what they think about themselves and you should weigh up what effect your appearance will have. Tailor your approach to the way you see your interviewee, not the way you see yourself. If you're in doubt about how your interviewee dresses, the safest option is to dress in a way that reflects the publication you represent. Otherwise opt for the style that will embarrass you least – being over- or under-dressed – and choose accordingly.

Planning the interview

It's vital to work out exactly what you want to know, how to approach your interviewee and the sort of questions you want to ask and this should not be hurried.

Whether the interview is to be on the telephone or in person, planning must start from an understanding of the publication and its readers. If you're a staff journalist you should already know your publication's editorial policy (what it is trying to achieve – inform, entertain, persuade, inspire, help, enthuse or whatever) and have a clear idea of who the readers are (their interests, why they buy the publication, how long they spend reading it, their interests and the vocabulary they feel happy with). If you're a freelance, you should work this out from a close reading of the publication.

Based on this, agree a preliminary working brief with your features editor. If the working brief has not been settled, then you have to decide who to interview and whether it's to be face to face or on the telephone.

Getting the brief right

The brief is the blueprint from which the feature is constructed. The relevant section for interviews includes the areas you intend to cover and what you are after: quotes, colour, anecdotes, background, information. These determine your approach and questions.

Research

Once the subject of the feature/interview and a preliminary brief have been agreed, start your research. If your subject is general – e.g., food hygiene regulations governing street markets or advice on editing parish magazines – you may need to do some research to discover articulate experts willing to talk. If your subject is already identified, say a politician or a star of a new TV soap, you will need to find out more about them and talk to their fans or detractors, agents or directors, partners, friends.

Look in the cuttings, on the Internet, in other publications, in books, encyclopedias. Talk to colleagues, contacts, friends, relations, neighbours, competitors, PRs, enemies. Check with the company, the organisation, the society; demand information anywhere and everywhere. Note what you find out and where you found it and always remember that information is only as good as the source. The Internet is not always reliable.

Suppose your subject is 'weather forecasting', a huge subject with a gigantic cast of characters. You could spend weeks, perhaps months, reading round the subject but you haven't the time. So start with a quick look at an official meteorological web site or an encyclopedia reference. Find the names of some experts and phone them. Somewhere there is someone who is, in effect, a search engine on the subject and can point you towards the most knowledgeable amateur, the most eccentric rainfall measurer in Iceland, the academic researching the most esoteric aspect of storms, TV weather forecasters in Papua New Guinea, etc.

Read everything you can, then pause. Turn yourself into your editor/features editor and your readers. What would they want to know? What questions address their interests/concerns? Pause again. Ask yourself what hasn't been covered? What doesn't hang together? Where are the gaps, the cracks? What questions hasn't this person answered yet? This is where the fresh, the unexpected question is formulated that yields the new, revealing, startling quote or fact. It's by knowing the old angle that you get the new angle.

Here's where the angle begins to emerge and you can start to firm up the brief. Lynda Lee-Potter had to interview the actress Diana Rigg, a notoriously difficult interviewee. Lee-Potter read all the cuttings, going back years, and decided there was one area which Rigg had never talked about: her childhood. That was the angle she pursued. She engaged Rigg's interest and obtained an excellent interview.

Inadequate research means you can miss the story. *Local Government Chronicle* commissioned freelance Janet Barber to interview the head of a local government organisation. She checked *Who's Who*, looked in the cuttings and prepared her questions. Back at the office after the interview she mentioned she'd just talked to him and a colleague said: 'Oh yes, he's the one who had a brick thrown through his window, isn't he?' Her man had been linked with a nationalist group, something she knew nothing about. 'So I had to phone him back, check and as a result got a much better interview. Now I check with as many sources as I can, particularly colleagues,' says Barber.

Sometimes her subjects turn out to be elusive. The most reluctant was John McGill, the district auditor who examined Westminster City Council's records during the Lady Porter investigation.

'He wouldn't talk to me. His firm [PricewaterhouseCoopers] wouldn't release any information about him, not one soupçon would they give me. The greatest initial help was looking him up in *Who's Who*, getting any printed biography at all.

Then I went round absolutely every single person connected with the case and everywhere he might have had any connection. I discovered he was the auditor for Surrey County Council and so got on to the director of finance there who gave me some helpful personal information. Press officers aren't always helpful. I sometimes feel they're like actors' agents, there to prevent you getting the information. The Internet's great here.'

The same happened with a Conservative Central Office official. As Barber recalls:

'It was an uphill task. The unhelpfulness of their press office was absolutely unbelievable. They would not give me any information at all. I tried colleagues. I had to ask around: does anybody know him? Do they know what he looks like?

I sat down and really worked the phone. I got lift-off when I finally found someone who knew him who was willing to talk on the record. I had to be able to quote people by name, at least three or four of them, though I used info from the rest as background.

In the end it made a cover story but we couldn't get a photo specially taken, we had to blow up a conference photo of him with someone else. Later one of my colleagues took him out to lunch and he said, "She managed very well, considering we wouldn't give her any help at all".'

What to ask

Research gives you the angle and points up the areas to cover. By this time you will have established what you want to know: what combination of information (facts, names, details), opinion (quotes), background (context), and/or anecdotes.

You must then work out what areas you want to cover, what questions you want to ask. Questions – formulating them, revising them, asking them – are discussed at length in Chapter 4. Interview pre-planning includes deciding what topics to cover/how many questions to prepare. As many as you think is right, with several left over for emergencies is safest. The number ranges from 25 to 60 for an hour. 'A question for every line in my notebook,' one journalist told me. If in doubt, err on the long side.

Obviously, you must discover your publication's 'must-know' facts: spelling of name, job title, exact name of employing company, annual turnover (for *Business Week* say); spelling of name, age, occupation and where they live (for a local paper); name, location, hectarage of farm, number/breed of cows in the herd (*Dairy Farmer*); price per square metre of carpet, fibre, manufacturer (*Floors and Floor Covering*), or whatever. Often exchanging business cards and reading annual reports yield much basic info. Then you need to work out how best to discover answers to the rest of the areas you wish to cover.

Write topics/questions down on a separate sheet of paper and, if you're doing a business interview needing replies to such questions as last year's turnover, percentage increase over previous year, exports by value, exports by volume, etc., it's a good idea to number these questions, then put that number against the answer during the interview. That avoids finding loads of statistics in your notebook but not having a clear memory of which question they were answers to.

Though it's vital to go into the interview with topics/questions prepared, it's equally vital to be ready to rephrase them to suit your interviewee once you're face to face. And never forget that all the time you're talking they're probably trying to work out how the interview will look in print. If they can't see any advantage to them, they may become cagey – the last thing you want.

When to arrive

Arrive on time or slightly early, even though you may be kept waiting. To be late is unforgivable, so when you set out, allow for possible delays.

Once, reporting for a Third World charity quarterly, I found the lift out of order and so had to walk up three flights of stairs. I've still not forgotten the shock of reaching fund-raiser James Tysoe's office as the hour struck and being shown straight in, puffing, without having collected my thoughts, my breath, double-checked where my notebook and pen were, or familiarised myself again with the questions I planned to ask. Flustered is not a good way to start an interview.

Obviously you can be more relaxed if you're driving down to Dorset to interview someone at their home. But tycoons, PRs running celebrity junkets, managers and business people all work to tight schedules and it's vital to be there for your slot or you may lose it.

If you are late, don't assume all is lost. The best way to avert wrath is to let them know en route that you've been held up. Which is why you have your mobile phone and their contact number with you.

And now . . .

You've done all your research and thought of a fresh and lively angle; you've prepared your topics/questions carefully and are ready to rephrase them to suit your interviewee; you've packed notebooks, pens, pencils, etc.; you know where you're going; you're dressed like the sort of person your interviewee will talk to.

You've set off in good time, making allowances for traffic and potential hold-ups. All your efforts must now concentrate on the interviewee. They are the star of the interview and anything, truly anything, that suggests you're not making them central to the encounter could damage, maybe even ruin, the interview.

Unless you're sure you can leave your packages in an outer office, don't arrive carrying shopping, parcels, a paperback novel even. The message it sends is the wrong one and establishing rapport is now your top imperative.

THE INTERVIEW STARTS

First impressions

First impressions count. TV dramatist Andrea Newman was once interviewed by seven journalists in one day. She says that by interviewer number five she knew in the first few seconds if the interview would work. One writer walked into the hall, sniffed dismissively and commented 'Ummmm.' It was a short interview.

Nerves and lack of practice handicap the beginner. To make a good first impression, it's necessary to get through the door in a pleasant but businesslike way. If you're seeing someone at their place of work, you may be asked to wait.

Resist all impulses to unpack your bag and recheck you've brought notebook, tape recorder, etc. Sod's law will spring into operation and, just as everything is scattered about, the interviewee will turn up in person. Settle down to wait, confident that you prepared well, and look forward to meeting your inter-viewee. It's wise to read any company literature offered and look around the reception area for clues to your interviewee or the company. Of course listen to any conversations going on around you.

You may be ushered in by a secretary or assistant, or may just be pointed at a door. Though the following advice sounds corny and like the PE teacher's warm-up routine, try it if you're at all nervous. As you approach the door, take a deep breath, stand tall and put your shoulders back.

If you're expected, there's no need to knock and wait. Walk in, right up to the interviewee. If you lurk close to the door you give off the wrong signal. You're there as a journalist, not a supplicant.

However anxious you are, walking in looking worried is counter-productive. Be pleased to see your interviewee. That means looking at them and smiling – and if you don't manage this naturally, perhaps you should rethink your career choice.

Shaking hands

The first anxiety for most beginners when face-to-face with their interviewee is about shaking hands. If your interviewee advances, hand outstretched, take it without hesitation. If your hand is clammy from nerves, brush or rub it dry on your trousers or skirt as you step forward.

Should the interviewee make no gesture either way, then it's up to you. Shaking hands seems sensible, since it can be revealing. Most handshakes are unremarkable but occasionally, if you interview businessmen for example, you may experience the truly surprising dominant, 'palm down' power shake. Your hand is grasped firmly, somehow turned palm up, then given a sharp shake. Weird.

There's also the 'politician's' handshake, where their two hands cover your one. This is usually diagnosed as a wish to project honesty. An add-on is the left hand grasping your elbow or upper arm at the same time, interpreted as a desire to convey honesty plus concern and warmth. Of course, some people have weak handshakes from necessity or for self-protection. They may have arthritis or need their hands to make a living: pianists, puppeteers, embroiderers or surgeons, for example.

Eye contact

How and how much you look at your interviewee matters vitally – look, please, not stare. Whether they realise it or not, it affects how much they will tell you. Look at them and they know they have your interest. Continue looking and they know they have your full attention, which is flattering. Conversely, look away at your notes or your questions, and they know you've ceased to concentrate on them.

Smile, too: a simple, unforced, pleased-to-meet-you smile. Smiling makes people who smile feel better, so it works in your favour, and it will also reassure your interviewee. An anxious scowl gets everything off to a poor start.

What to call them? If in doubt it's safer to be formal – 'Mr', 'Mrs' or 'Ms'. Some interviewees loathe informality and using their first name straightaway prejudices them against you immediately. If they're happy with informality they'll soon let you know. Only one more ritual to observe. If you haven't already done so, introduce yourself, giving your name and publication.

Where to sit

Don't be in a hurry at this stage. Certainly don't sit down until you're asked to. Take your time before you begin. One good way to start is to thank the interviewee for seeing you. Some journalists won't do this on principle, reasoning that the interviewee isn't doing them a favour but hoping to gain from the transaction. However, from the journalist's viewpoint it's a wise move. Like smiling, it suggests interest and pleasure. It reassures the nervous and encourages the uncertain.

If this is your first interview, sit where indicated. Later, with growing experience and confidence you can be more choosy, because where you sit matters. Accepted wisdom is that sitting directly opposite your interviewee is a mistake. It's confrontation, the chess or 'war' position.

Sitting too far away is a mistake too, as is sitting next to each other on the sofa. This is gruesomely matey and pure agony if you use shorthand or combined tape recorder and notes, since the interviewee has only to throw in a few statistics, names or brand names to see exactly what you're taking down and how far behind you are.

There's general agreement that sitting at or around right-angles (90°) works best, being neither too confrontational nor too cosy. As you grow more confident, with business interviews especially, avoid any chair that's lower than your interviewee's since that puts you in a subordinate position. No need for the converse advice – it won't happen.

If, when you're a more experienced interviewer, you are directed to a seat on the executive sofa and wish to avoid it, say something along the lines of: 'If it's OK with you, I'd prefer to sit . . .' (indicating where). Only the truly cussed interviewee would object.

At ease

Your next task is to build rapport, which is easier than it sounds. You started when you greeted them warmly and thanked them for agreeing to see you. Now you need to say something that makes them look kindly on you.

The easiest way to build rapport is to establish common ground: to mention some thing, experience, attitude or belief you both share and agree on. There's no one sure method. It varies from interviewee to interviewee. If you know from their CV that they went to the same university you did, say so. You went to Bristol/Oxford/Manchester/York/London University? You're more than OK. You come with a positive stamp of approval.

If their company has just pulled off a major acquisition against long odds, offer congratulations. Praise, aka flattery, never goes amiss. If the view from the window is stunning, say so. If they have a Burmese cat, and your auntie has one too, tell them. Establish a community of likes. Make yourself agreeable in a way that shows you see them as an interesting person, not just a potential source to be squeezed dry of facts in as short a time as possible.

As you become more experienced, there's another way to establish rapport: mirror their body language. If they sit back relaxed, you sit back relaxed. If they lean forward, you lean forward. If they cross their legs, you cross your legs. It needs to be subtly done. Don't try this until you're at ease with the interview process or you'll do it clumsily and it will be so obvious it won't work; like the synchronised swimming team's first practice session, in fact.

Matching the interviewee's rate of speaking also works, both to establish rapport and to make the interview flow smoothly throughout, and this is easier to achieve.

When to begin

It's said that most people make up their minds about a person in the first four minutes after being introduced, so a mixture in that time of charm and getting down to business is recommended – unless the discussion about the university, take-over, view or cat is going so well it would be crass to interrupt. Your interviewee may be quite nervous and need time to settle down or may prattle away confidently from the first. Either way, sooner or later – and you must be the judge of when – there will come a time when you must begin. It's your interview.

You are *and must be* in charge. However subtly it's done, you call the shots. If you don't, you may end up writing at their dictation or being borne off on a flood of useless reminiscence, unable to stop the flow. For some fact-heavy, structured interviews, the control needs to be tight but many interviewers find they get the best quotes by using a firm hand in a very velvety glove. You walked through the door knowing what you wanted to get out of the interview. It is up to you whether you walk out mission accomplished or not.

Down to business

Time to get out your notebook or tape recorder. Unless you're dealing with someone who's very nervous, there's no need to apologise or ask permission. If you have any doubts say something like 'No objection to a tape recorder, I hope.' Make it a statement rather than a question. Now's the time, too, to give them your business card if you have one.

Before launching into the interview, you should remind them what you want to talk about. This is true whether they are a top-flight professional doing six interviews a day or being interviewed for the first time. Repeating the interview subject and angle focuses their minds. It's in your interest that they know. If they don't, they may set off in what for you is a hopeless direction, wasting everyone's time.

Rather than a brusque 'OK, tell me about your snail farm', a softer and wiser approach would be to explain some of the thinking behind the interview. For example:

> 'Farmers' Week readers are very interested in diversification and your snail farm is one of the most unusual ideas we've heard about. I'm hoping you can give me a picture of where you got the idea, about your start-up and running costs, the pleasures and pitfalls of snail farming and if you'd recommend it to other farmers. That sort of thing.'

The idea is to avoid an abrupt jump start, to give them a little time to collect their thoughts and get ready to answer. Everyone is advised to start gently. If you ask something your interviewee can't answer, they may feel cross with themselves and, most likely, furious with you too. Either way it's a bad idea.

For several reasons, beginners are advised to start with their 'must-know' facts. First, because these are safe and easy to confirm. Second, because they reassure the interviewee, dealing as they do with accurate checking. Third, because by the end of the interview the first-time interviewer may be so exhausted or elated they forget to ask. It happens. And so does the embarrassing follow-up phone call. 'Hello, it's . . . again. Sorry to bother you, but I forgot to check . . .'

Again, don't start abruptly. Plunging in with: 'What's your name and how do you spell it?' isn't recommended. Much better, as suggested in the next chapter, is to say: 'I'd like to start by checking how you spell your name.' You're aiming for an interview that runs smoothly, where your interviewee feels at ease.

Make it interesting – for them

Empathy, rather than sympathy, is a prime requirement for interviewers. Until you've been interviewed by a succession of journalists relentlessly pumping you for information or quotes, you can have no idea how boring being asked the same questions can be – especially if the answers elicit no response except the next, predictable question.

Shirley Conran, an accomplished self-publicist, went round the world promoting her books and said about her first bestseller, Lace, that interviewers only ever asked four questions – and one of them was 'always about the goldfish.' So be sure to make the interview a pleasure for your subject. This means engaging their interest from the start. Early on ask something that shows you're not just another hack, routinely asking the obvious questions.

Doctors have 'heart-sink' patients, who visit the surgery every day – the doctor's heart sinks at the sight of them. Avoid being a 'heart-sink' questioner, signalling from the beginning that the interview is to cover well-trampled ground. The interviewee subconsciously switches off, gives well-rehearsed answers and functions on automatic pilot – exactly what shouldn't happen.

4
Interviewing techniques

Here's that rare thing, a chapter on interviewing techniques that doesn't start with questions. That's because the main purpose of a print interview is to get the interviewee talking freely and the best way to do that is to listen.

As American writer John Brady put it: 'No talking journalist ever held a good interview.' The description of an interview as 'a conversation with a purpose' is misleading, unless what's in mind is a cleverly guided, very one-sided conversation.

Interviewers need to master the non-questioning skills of eliciting information and quotes. These are to:

- listen and encourage;
- use silence;
- make statements requiring confirmation/denial;
- summarise and move on.

There is good reason for this apparently perverse order, starting as it does with the 'mute' techniques. Listening and encouraging people to talk are not the simple skills they seem. If not learnt and practised early, they may fall into dangerous neglect. Worse, journalists raised on TV and radio interviews who have received little or no specialist training may not even believe they exist and instead adopt the rapid-fire, ping-pong Q & A style quite wrong for print journalists.

The first injunction is to be flexible. The aim is to get your interviewee to drop their defences. This means you have to adapt your approach to suit them – calm the excitable, reassure the uncertain and steer the confident and knowledgeable.

Good interviewers are long-time people watchers and eavesdroppers. They look, they listen. They ask themselves: what does that gesture mean; why did that person look down then; why such a dramatic response to such a casual question; are those two squaring up for a row; why doesn't she interrupt him;

who's the dominant person in that group; what do those three have in common?

If they can, they stick around to check if their answers are right. Fans of the movies score well here, as do actors turned writers, for obvious reasons. They listen, they watch, they analyse.

If there's one motto that interviewers should adopt it's *You get more flies with honey than vinegar*. Being nice works better than being nasty almost every time and certainly to begin with.

Listen and encourage

One of life's ironies is that of the four great communicating skills – listening, speaking, reading and writing – the one that is learnt first, listening, is taught least, while writing, which is learnt last, is taught most. Listening requires immense concentration and is exhausting. Anyone aiming for an interview longer than an hour is advised to take a break, for their own sake as well as the interviewee's.

Listening also requires empathy, discipline, understanding and patience. If you're tense, indifferent, hostile, impatient or distracted you won't listen well. The best listeners, rather like the best reportage photographers, are self-effacing. They concentrate on their interviewees so much that they almost become invisible. One sign of a good interviewer is that you're forgotten.

Listening is not the same as hearing. Good listening is hearing *and* understanding. In face-to-face interviews it means you are interested in what's being said and show it clearly, so you should look at your interviewee. Although it's possible to listen to someone with your back to them, they will hate it and, being uncertain of your attention, will dry up.

Interviewees won't maintain steady eye contact with you but they need to know when they check back – as they do at irregular intervals – that you're concentrating on them. Lynda Lee-Potter says if you take your eyes off them for even a split second you can hear their voices start to falter. Celebrities often have a greater need than most to be looked at because they're used to it.

Once you have got people talking, you need to encourage them to continue. This means using reassuring body language: mirroring their posture in the first place, using nods, head tilts, leaning forward, smiling. Mirroring their posture is subliminal reassurance. Nods are much more noticeable, a sign that you hear and understand. Nods usually come singly or in pairs. Three is overdoing it and usually signals that you wish to interrupt. If you're not a natural nodder, watch others, practise and, before you add nodding to your interview techniques, check how comfortable you look in a mirror. Too many forced nods look ridiculous and inhibit rather than encourage your interviewee.

The vocalised version, the 'uh-huh' – often accompanied by an almost invisible nod – is another great encourager. It's very useful in face-to-face interviews and essential on the telephone. Used liberally, it helps answers to flow freely. The American version of the British 'uh-huh' is 'uh-*ah*', which rises on the last syllable and is much more upbeat than the grunt. Used repeatedly, as verbal encouragers tend to be during interviews, 'uh-huh' is definitely preferable to repeatedly spoken single or double-words such as 'right', 'yes', 'I see', 'that so?' Singly, they work. Too many and they become a huge irritant.

Head tilts – putting your head on one side – come naturally to some. They're a way of saying 'Please carry on'. If you watch people listening to young children you'll see head tilts most of the time. The listener silently encourages the child to continue, sending out an 'I'm hearing you' message.

Leaning forward is another way of showing how engaged you are. Like mirroring the interviewee's body language, it broadcasts a subconscious approval message. Smiling adds further reassurance. The opposite of all these, an impassive, non-responsive, stony-faced interviewer sends out all the wrong messages – messages certain to be received at some level.

Use silence

It's impossible to over-emphasise the importance of silence. Not in the first few minutes of the interview, of course, when you're establishing your credentials, or if you have a nervous, over-talkative interviewee, but once they have taken your measure, relaxed and started to talk easily, then you must talk very little.

It's difficult to be silent – agin nature for some journalists – but it's one of the most valuable techniques. So get into the habit of not jumping in with another question or comment as soon as the interviewee has finished speaking. Instead, count at least four seconds silently to yourself. You'll be amazed how often the interviewee carries on speaking, amplifying their last comment. Most of us discover this for the first time when we are stumped for what to ask next, and are astonished to find our interviewee doesn't seem to have realised but carries on speaking as though nothing has happened.

For those who are unsure how long four seconds lasts, it's about the time you can say to yourself 'One Mississippi, two Mississippi, three Mississippi, four Mississippi'. However ill at ease you feel, persevere. I opted for a four-second pause several years ago, mostly on a gut-feel. It seemed the right amount of time to allow before continuing. It was gratifying to learn while researching this book, that three seconds is the time it takes most people to frame replies. Don't over-do it, though, and use really long silences. They're counter-productive, leading to short answers.

If you need extra persuasion to keep silent, bear in mind that the more you interrupt, the less you listen and the less they will talk. What to listen for? Everything, really. First, the exact words the interviewee uses, then their eagerness or reluctance to answer particular questions, the tone or strength of voice, any pauses, omissions, where they become animated, where they sound reluctant and on and on.

Listening to precisely what is said is particularly important if the interviewee is well practised in dealing with journalists. In these days of sophisticated news management, many interviewees are trained in how to respond to unwelcome questions. They know that the truth and nothing but the truth is easy but that the whole truth is the killer. So given a choice between lying, fudging, evading or telling the truth, the adept will opt for a limited amount of the truth, because it's easy to remember and a great protection. That's why listening to *exactly* what they say is essential.

> 'We finance 15 overseas scholarship places a year.'
> Don't presume 15 scholarships have been awarded.

> 'The chairman studied archaeology at Cambridge.'
> Don't presume he or she got a degree in archaeology. They may have studied it but failed finals.

> 'Our budget? Well, it's under a million.'
> This last from a producer replying to queries about his first film which had a budget of £11,000.

The story is told about General de Gaulle, questioned after Britain had devalued the pound and there was heavy pressure on France to follow suit. Under questioning, he said he would devalue the franc by somewhere between 0 per cent and 5 per cent. This answer bought him and the franc time, and pressure for action eased. He then did exactly what he had said: he devalued by 0 per cent.

One clue to the limited-truth reply is that the interviewee often rephrases the question in answering. Suppose it is:

> 'When was the first time you heard he'd quit as manager?'

and the answer is:

> 'I was gobsmacked to hear him talking about it on the radio on Monday morning.'

The statement may be true but it doesn't answer the question. Politicians are great exponents of rephrasing when answering as it enables them to answer a different question smoothly.

Listening attentively is an obvious compliment to the interviewee. It also allows you to collect the information you're after and ask intelligent supplementary questions. The converse – not paying attention, not asking obvious follow-up questions but rather ones that are random and inconsequential – offends interviewees and is one of the prime reasons for interviews being cut short.

You should listen particularly for changes in the strength of voice or speed of talking. Dropping or lowering tone and slowing down usually mean you've reached something significant about which the interviewee has reservations of some sort, usually emotional. Raising or increasing the volume generally signifies positive, tell-the-world content.

Make statements requiring confirmation/ denial

Questioning sits on a continuum that ranges from casual checking at one end to interrogating at the other. Considering the power of the press, it's easy to understand why many people are apprehensive before being interviewed.

One way to put them at their ease is not to ask questions but to seek confirmation. You can do this through statements.

> 'I'd just like to check how you spell your name.'

This is a much better opener than the brusque:

> 'How do you spell your name?'

Similarly:

> 'I see from the cuttings that you have a house in the south west of France.'

Or

> 'Friends tell me you have a house in the Charente, in the south west.'

Gathering information this way is a knack that can take some time to acquire. The tone is generally softer and more friendly.

> 'You must have worked very hard to complete the refurbishment ahead of schedule and under budget.'

> 'Your customers say your sausages are the finest in Bawtry.'

> 'I called your colleague Helen, who tells me I must ask about your trip to the South Pole.'

> 'I understand it was your idea to develop the micro skate scooter.'

Getting information confirmed usually reassures interviewees that you're getting your facts right, but if you are trying to get them to confirm something not to their advantage, then a question is often wiser. It is easier to avoid responding to a statement such as:

'I understand there have been a lot of redundancies announced recently'

than it would be to answer the question:

'How many redundancies will there be?'

The guideline here is not to ask questions like this until well into the interview, when the interviewee is talking freely and senses that any avoidance or hesitation would send out a glaring signal of reluctance.

It's also possible to discover information by making statements that require denial and this is much more problematic, because you don't know what negative buttons you are pressing.

'There's no smoke without fire so I take it the rumour that your latest model has hit safety problems is true.'

'I understand you were once convicted of being drunk and incapable.'

Negative statements can often provoke a lively, vigorous denial but be sure of your interviewee before you try this too often.

Summarise and move on

One last and valuable type of statement is the summary. Use this when your interviewee is over-talkative. Summarise what they have said, restate it and then you can move on.

'So what you're saying is . . . Now I'd like to turn to . . .'

'Let's see if I've got this right . . . Perhaps we can now talk about . . .'

'We've covered . . . so next . . .'

QUESTIONS

Questions should be framed to achieve their purpose. Maybe it's to reassure the interviewee that you'll spell the name of their company correctly. Maybe it's to signal to them that you know more about their past than they suspect. Maybe it's to encourage them to talk about their favourite subject. Maybe it's to ensure they remember you.

As so often, Lynn Barber gets it right. 'Clever questions ... are a waste of time: the really clever question is the shortest one that will elicit the longest, most interesting answer – in practice usually "Why?"'

The intelligence behind the questions is vital and so is how you phrase and ask them. ITN's political editor John Sergeant, interviewed in *Press Gazette*, described one of his first journalistic assignments. He'd just joined the Liverpool *Daily Post* and was sent to cover a fatal industrial accident.

> 'I put down my pad as aggressively as I could muster and said: "Right, let's get the details" – and of course they wouldn't give anything away. Then the chief reporter arrived ... looking like Columbo with his old mac on. His approach to the manager was: "I suppose you won't be saying anything about this? Quite, I quite understand."

> But then he had this wonderful way of asking questions without appearing to. Within two minutes he had already framed the first four or five para-graphs. "I suppose he wouldn't have been here long ...? Oh, it was his first day.'

> I was just standing there gobsmacked ... You learn a lot about not being demanding and aggressive, not looking as if you knew the answers.'

Categories and categorising

You can categorise questions a number of ways – by purpose, by content, by way of asking – but first let's examine the three recognised main categories: closed, open and leading. All are valuable used at the right time.

Closed

These are commonly defined as questions that can be answered 'yes' or 'no' but more sensibly as questions about fact or opinion that can be answered briefly. Closed questions are ideal for establishing essential statistics, names, job titles, locations, once the interview is under way.

> 'Did you see the accident?'
> 'No.'

> 'Are you on email?'
> 'Yes.'

> 'What's the group's full title?'
> 'The United Bellringers of Scourie.'

> 'How many boats can anchor at the Marina?'
> '120.'

'What's her middle name?'
'Arabella.'

'Where was the last AGM held?'
'Birmingham.'

Closed questions can be useful if you're very near deadline as they speed up replies but using too many damps down the interviewee's interest. They move into answering, not talking, mode. The more closed questions are asked, the shorter the answers to any subsequent open questions will be.

The only people who seem to welcome closed questions are the inarticulate and the nervous with nothing to hide. Too many short answers do not a good interview make.

Open

Open questions require more than a few words for a satisfactory answer:

'How did the man saw through the bars using just dental floss?'

'What made you decide to become a Salvation Army officer?'

'Why do you think the pony survived being struck by lightning?'

'Exactly what is the difference between Spanish and Moroccan green olives?'

Among variations of the open question is the *echo*, to be used when you sense that the interviewee might like to say more, but that direct probing might not draw it out. Use this sparingly and practise first.

'I went absolutely ballistic.'
[Pause]
'You went absolutely ballistic?'

'I fell in love with him there and then.'
[Pause]
'You fell in love with him there and then?'

Amplification questions are a sub-category of open questions used to elicit detailed extra information. The task here is to get the interviewee to give specific examples – the valuable 'for instances' that are the hooks of communication.

'Then I started work for a Third World charity.'
'What exactly did the job involve?'
'Visiting community development schemes in Zambia and Brazil, talking to the families involved and reporting back to the supporters. I've slept in mud huts in Zambia, helped dispense condoms at an AIDS clinic and been inside two Brazilian brothels.'

'As a result, the two of them had a dreadful row.'
'Could you tell me more – for instance, were they shouting?'
'Shouting? They were screaming at each other. Richard called Andrew an upper-class prat and Andrew said Richard couldn't find his arse in the dark. Andrew walked out and hasn't been seen since. Richard's confiscated Andrew's mobile and instructed security not to let him into the building.'

'The company's had several bright marketing ideas.'
'Could you describe the three most successful to me?'

Clarification questions are another sub-category. The more you interview, the more you realise how important it is to check you've understood what you've been told.

'The outcome was so unfair I decided to leave there and then.'
'Is that when you went to work on the dictionary?'
'No, no, you misunderstand. I left work early that day. I didn't quit the job until later. I was headhunted by Mutel-Morange Ltd.'
'That was the same year?'
'No – it took a year before I moved.'

The approach here should be along the lines of:

'So what you're saying is . . .?'

'Would I be right that you think . . .?'

Because words mean different things to different people it's wise to check.

'She's prevaricating.'
'Do you mean she's putting things off or that she's lying?'
'She's definitely stalling.'

'I'm determined to go on being celibate.'
'Do you mean you'll not have sex – or that you won't marry?'
'Give up sex, of course.'

Beginners must get into the habit of asking clarification questions. It is far too easy to misunderstand what is being said as a result of mishearings, wrong construction, different ways of thinking, vocabulary being used differently by different age groups (e.g. 'It's wicked . . .').

Good open questions catch the interviewee's interest and unlock a wealth of information and opinion, encouraging them to talk freely because the interviewer appears interested in their views. The difficulty is that the interviewee may talk too much and swerve off on an unwelcome tangent, which is why for most interviews making it clear initially what you are after is so important.

Leading

Because they can usually be answered shortly, leading questions can be categorised as a sub-section of closed questions.

'You're a Lib Dem, aren't you?'

'How did you react? Were you furious?'

'How much money went missing – more than £250,000?'

'Did the accident happen just after they left the pub?'

Leading questions have a bad reputation, but they're much used in everyday conversation and experience shows that if the interviewee likes the questioner, they have little effect on the answers unless the suggested answer is way off beam.

Much more annoying can be the *assumptive* sub-category of leading questions, as in 'When did you stop beating your wife?'

'Are you married or single?'
'Neither, I'm divorced!'

'Did you come by bus or train?'
'I walked.'

But as before, if the assumption is correct, these questions work well because they demonstrate understanding and interest.

'You love the sea.'
'Yes – with a passion. What made you say that?'
'That photo of the yacht on your bookcase.'

'I've heard you love opera – I guess Verdi in particular.'
'Yes – how did you know?'
'Just a feeling.'

This last comment may be because everything said so far showed an emotional maturity plus an interest in the workings of the human heart – perhaps it was in the cuttings.

Sometimes during very tricky interviews using an assumptive question is one way to provoke an answer.

'When was the last time you smoked a spliff?'

Asking an assumptive question that relates back to something said at an earlier stage of the interview can flatter the interviewee, reinforcing how interesting their comments are. Referring back and getting it wrong can lead to a complicated and useful correction but don't try this too often or they suspect you're not as shrewd as they first thought.

'So when you said earlier the samples taken from the reservoir passed all the required tests, that means the water quality has been maintained at the same standard since the reservoir was built?'

'No, no – you can't assume that. The test standards were lowered in 1992. Take, for example, the requirements for testing for e-coli . . .'

Indirect assumptive questions are useful when you need to overcome a barrier. Best known is the classic

'How many raffle tickets would you like?'

instead of

'Would you like any raffle tickets?'

So:

'How many redundancies will there be?'

Not:

'Will there be any redundancies?'

Directive, suggestive or loaded

These are unattractive and manipulative, not recommended but regularly used by unfortunate journalists who have to return with quotes to fit a pre-set formula, slot into a known space or support a management opinion.

'You're happy to feed your child Frankenstein foods, not knowing what appalling deformities might result in years to come?'

'It's undeniable that 20mph zones save lives, so why should selfish, speeding motorists be listened to?'

'Mother Theresa [the Pope, Princess Diana, Mickey Mouse] said love was the most important thing in the universe. Don't you agree?'

'What sort of mother wouldn't support our campaign to have the names and addresses of local paedophiles published?'

Short, simple, clear

Since the first interview requirement is to communicate, common sense dictates that short questions are better than long ones, simple questions better than convoluted ones, clear questions better than abstruse ones. Common sense may dictate this but, alas, common sense is a rare commodity. This is where using a tape recorder and listening back to interviews is embarrassingly instructive.

When it comes to broad or narrow, objective or subjective questions, there can be no pat answer. The guideline is to make the question relevant to your requirements and to the interviewee.

Cautious, legalistic minds dislike broad questions.

> 'What did you think of Australia?'
> 'In what way? Do you want to know my reaction to the people, the scenery, the wine, what exactly?'

The more relaxed and less exact would have no such worries.

> 'Wonderful place. Loved it, especially crossing the Nullabor plain by train, fireworks in Sydney on new year's eve, kangaroos and parrots on the golf course. And the natives were friendly – especially when Australia were beating us at cricket.'

If you're after a lot of information, move carefully from broad brush to detailed follow-ups, particularly if the subject is at all wary. Long, complicated follow-up questions immediately after a broad general question signal that there's a lot of very detailed questioning to follow and if time is short and you are less than endearing, the interview may end swiftly. Consider this scenario:

> 'Have you ever lived in Cambodia?'
> 'Yes. For six months, really loved it.'

There follows a long list of questions wanting detailed information about the standard of accommodation, food, buses, trains, weather, shops. All are answered patiently.

> 'Have you ever lived in Laos?'
> 'Yes. For two months . . .'

Same long list of questions follow. Interviewee is less patient.

> 'Have you lived in China?'
> 'No.'
> 'Or Thailand?'
> 'Never!'

The advice is to ask all general questions first, then go back and obtain the details you want.

Customise your questions

Make your questions suit your interviewee. People who are at home with facts and figures, people who are well-defended or pompous or tentative or scared usually resist hypothetical questions. The creative, by contrast, welcome the 'what would you do if . . . ?' approach and will freewheel away into fantasy, which can make for good copy.

More than that, make your questions exact and precise. Enthusiasm makes for good quotes, so if your research shows that your interviewee has a passion for quattrocento (15th-century Italian) art, frame an exact question.

> 'If you had to choose one picture that sums up all you love about quattrocento art, which would it be – and why?'

Or if your interviewee is a noted vegetarian celebrity:

> 'If you were planning a gourmet vegetarian meal – what would you cook and who would you invite?'

Hopping between objective and subjective questions – queries about observable facts or happenings and about personal opinions and views – can be very disturbing for interviewees, particularly those who think exactly, logically and slowly. Only the disorganised and/or creative can cope.

Avoid interrogation

There's a school of interviewing that recommends interviewers adopt a variety of stances from investigator and confessor to inquisitor and judge. But investigators often operate under cover, confessors behind a screen, inquisitors have recourse to torture, and judges require people on oath.

In other words, don't. Always try to interview person to person, adult to adult, eyeball to eyeball. Neither abase nor elevate yourself, unless your interviewee will not talk otherwise. In these egalitarian days, being condescended to is appalling and being venerated wearying.

Interviewers who see themselves as attorneys for the public, intimidating and cross-examining their interviewees into a state of gibbering incoherence, do nothing for journalism, says Anthony Howard of the *Times*. Soothing interviewers have much more success. 'A good bedside manner,' he says, 'is still the best way to elicit a scoop.'

Beguile not browbeat

Clive James believes that the adversarial style is

> 'pretty nearly useless even when you interview a real adversary. If I had asked Ronald Reagan: "*Were* you a stoolie for the FBI in Hollywood?" he would have told me nothing. I asked him: "How serious *was* the Communist threat in Hollywood?" and he told me everything, implicating himself up to the eyebrows.'

One of the most beguiling interviewers I ever watched at work was on the staff of an obscure trade publication. Interviewees said being interviewed by him was like being wrapped in a fur bedspread – soft, silky and strangely seduc-tive. They felt impelled to answer his questions because they sensed it mattered so much to him.

If you're interviewing on a sensitive subject – money, sex, relationships, educa-tion (never forget that to many people their lack of qualifications is a very sensitive matter indeed) – do not be embarrassed or judgmental. That sends out all the wrong messages and your interviewees will sense your attitude and in turn feel embarrassed or furious. Be straightforward, don't use euphemisms, avoid judgmental words. No questions involving 'unconventional tendencies', 'surprising impulses' or 'facing up to problems'. Be matter-of-fact.

Every journalist I've met who has ever done a sex interview started by thinking it would be difficult and discovered the only problem was shutting the inter-viewee up. You usually learn more than you expect, sometimes more than you wish. Interviewing the vulnerable is a very different matter requiring a different approach (see p. 137).

Telling trio

You need only three questions, it's said. These vary according to source. For the composer Brahms they were: 'Whence? Wherefore? Whither?' ITN's polit-ical editor John Sergeant says they're: 'How bad is it? Is it getting worse? So what can be done?' A newspaper version is: 'When did this start? And then? What of the future?' These are, in effect, questions to discover the beginning, the middle and the end of a story – the basis of all journalism. So when trying to find out the beginning, middle and end of the story, please remember it's the quality and freshness of the questions which matter.

For a charity promotion, journalists interviewed a man who planned to walk all round the British coast. When would he set off, they asked; what was his route; how long it would take; where he would stay; how much would he raise for charity? – all routine stuff he'd answered many times before. Then someone asked: 'What about your *feet*?' And at that point he perked up, the pack perked up and the story took off.

Useful questions

Here, then, are questions that have worked for a variety of journalists. There's no such thing as a never-fail question but there are some reliables. These include old faithfuls like:

'What's the best/worst. . . .?'

'If you had two minutes on national TV . . .'

'Who's been the greatest influence on you?'

'Do you have a pet hate?'

Part of the function of a book like this is to offer examples of different questions for consideration but please, when you interview, ask questions in your own words – otherwise you'll be like the unfortunate salespeople who have to work from a script – not happy, not convincing and not very successful.

To an interviewee speaking in jargon:
'How would you explain that to a layman?'

For any successful person:
'Have you any advice for youngsters just setting out?'

For business or political interviews where you've just heard a controversial opinion and/or inflated claim:
'What evidence do you have for that?'

If you meet someone on a factory visit, at a press conference, visiting a local organisation and you can't remember their name:
'Remind me how you spell your name again.'

For any high-flying business person:
'How come you, of all the company's 10,000 [or whatever] employees, made it to the top?'

For people still climbing the ladder:
'What drives/motivates you?'

There is a remarkable set of questions devised by Eric Berne, author of *Games People Play*, in his book *What Do You Say After You Say Hello?* They link in with the Parent/Adult/Child approach of transactional analysis. Here's a selection:

'What will it say on the front of your tombstone?'

'If your family were put on the stage, what sort of play would it be?'

'What did your parents forbid you to do?'

'Do you ever lie awake at night planning revenge?'

'How far ahead do you begin to worry about things?'

'What will your last words be?'

A set of hypothetical questions to ask an articulate interviewee who's in rare form:

You meet a man at the end of the world and he asks you three questions which you have to answer spontaneously and immediately. The first is: 'Who are you?'

[Pause for answer]

The second question is: 'Apart from that who are you?'

[Pause for answer]

And the last is: 'Apart from *that* who are you?'

A variation on that approach is to ask

'If you *had* to find a needle in a haystack, how would you do it?'

Answers to this question are said to reveal the root of your being:

'Hire someone to do it for me,' said an economist.

'Burn it down and use a metal detector,' said a powerful businessman.

'Use a giant magnet,' said a playwright.

If your interviewee shows signs of wanting to go and you're sure there's much more to come:

'Am I boring you?'

Said to guarantee 20 extra minutes.

To an interviewee who refuses to give a direct answer to a pointed question and squirms around, fudging his or her replies:

'I'll take it that's a yes.'

Almost every newspaper or magazine Q&A feature has some questions that can be used for a general profile interview.

'What books are on your bedside table?'

'What really pisses you off?'

'If you could make one change to the world/your company/your town/ village/club – with money no object, what would it be?'

'What's your motto?'

'Where do you expect to be in five years' time?'

'How do you handle disappointment?'

'What makes you feel important?'

'What's the most important lesson you've learnt in life?'

'Who's your hero?'

'What three words would you use to describe yourself?'

'If you were a biscuit, what sort would you be?'

'If you knew you were going to die tomorrow what would you do tonight?'

Softly, softly

Skilful interviewers can ask almost anybody anything and get a reasonable response. Approach and style are what counts. You can ask tough or rude questions if you ask in the right away.

The really offensive questions are those that relate to what people can't change – their height, the colour of their skin, physical abnormalities. But even those can be asked sympathetically once the interview is under way. Lynda Lee-Potter took 45 minutes to ask an interviewee if she took her artificial leg off at night. When Lee-Potter judged the time was right, she received a slightly puzzled answer: 'Yes, of course.'

You need to be seen as sympathetic and understanding by the person you're talking to. They must feel they can trust you. Luckily, there is a role model accessible to UK journalists. Sue Lawley on *Desert Island Discs* questions people about murders they've committed, suicide attempts, disasters in their careers, bitter divorces. Well briefed, gentle and calm, she brings up the subject, asks the question and waits for an answer. The emotional temperature is cool. There's no forced jollity or mateyness, simply a space for the interviewee to answer.

Robert McCrum, the *Observer*'s literary editor, was a *Desert Island Discs* castaway and wrote a feature about it, which captures a central point about being interviewed. 'I would . . . happily have spent all day discussing the infinitely fascinating subject of Me.'

Start nice . . .

If you want to ask important questions that you sense your interviewee will not wish to answer, approach gently and if you meet refusal, anger or aggression, quickly veer away – apologising if that's your style – returning to the subject later.

If you want to ask questions that you *know* will cause trouble, common sense dictates that you leave them until the end when you have the bulk of the interview in your notebook or on tape. Then, if thrown out, you can still write the story.

Lynn Barber, however, recommends asking a tough question near the start of the interview. She argues that 'the subject's relief at having survived it so quickly and painlessly may pay dividends for the rest of the interview.' That this approach works for her is a tribute to her prodigious interviewing skills.

Much depends on whether it's *a* tough question or *the* tough question. Compare Barber's approach with that of Andrew Duncan (p. 117) who leaves the 'A' question hovering unasked until the interviewee almost begs it to be put.

Warn of a change of tack

With a few exceptions – for example, those you are trying to wrong-foot or trap – the best way to ask an unpleasant question is to give fair warning. You tell your interviewee you are going to ask a difficult/hard/rude/impertinent/offensive question and then you do. Because they are prepared, the sting goes out of the question and they feel more able – and more obliged – to answer. Try it.

> 'I know it's daft, but journalists always have to put the age in – so how old are you?'

> 'This may be really offensive, but why – when you work in such a sober business – do you wear such cheesy ties?'

> 'I know you're important and run a department with a budget of several millions, but why did you put your feet on the desk right now?'

> 'This may sound rude, but you're 45, a mother of four and working with people whose lives are wrecked – so why the *Star Trek* watch?'

> 'This may be too difficult to answer – but how come such an untidy person ever managed to write a book?'

Other approaches with difficult questions

First: make the question very simple. This is highly recommended for well-protected, skilled and tricky interviewees.

> 'Will you explain why you are not implementing your planned factory expansion?'

No criticism, no loaded words, no added details, no named sources for the interviewee to latch on to and attack. This approach makes it difficult for interviewees to dodge, divert or rubbish the question.

Second: lay the blame elsewhere.

> 'Your detractors say your company has a reputation for going in for cartels, tax avoidance – things people think multinationals shouldn't do. Do you think that's fair criticism?

This allows you to ask a tough question but offers your interviewee the chance to see it as enabling them to counter hostile allegations.

Third: soften with schmooze; preface the attack with praise.

> 'Your latest movie has won five Oscar nominations and is doing great business at the box office – but isn't the bidet scene really, really tacky?'

Fourth: treat it lightly by implying the question is not so serious.

> 'I'd like to play devil's advocate here and look at what you did from a different angle. Then the question becomes – why did you put your name forward, considering your track record?'

Fifth: try separate, apparently disconnected questions. A two-step approach.

> 'You've always been idealistic, haven't you? I know you support animal welfare charities and would never wear fur. I'm right there, aren't I?'

The questioner already knows the answer to these two questions, then follows them up with:

> 'So why do you send your children to a fee-paying school when you believe in equality of opportunity?'

Good humour, humour and cheek

Good humour in an interviewer is a great plus unless your interviewee is pompously self-important. A cheerful approach helps interviewees relax. It also can prevent and/or defuse anger, deflect aggression and lighten intense situations.

In most interviews, humour works wonders. No book can help you here, you're on your own. But if you've got the ability to make people laugh, use it. Amid the serious business of information extraction, making a cheeky comment is the equivalent of a feint in judo. It changes the dynamics and gives you the initiative.

Another plus. If you make your interviewee laugh, you move out of the questioning slot. Two provisos: know your own deficiencies – not everyone can tell a joke or an anecdote successfully. Second, ensure your interviewee is laughing *with* you.

Flattery

It's deeply worrying how much flattery people can absorb. It rarely goes amiss, because it makes them feel valued, reassures them all is well and with luck gets them to drop their defences.

'I loved your book – it was marvellous, particularly the part . . .'

If the interviewee has written a book, you must read it if you have time or know something more about it than the title if time is short.

'You always give me such really wonderful and vivid quotes.'

Try this even if their quotes are not particularly outstanding, because one of the great things about people is that performance often rises to meet expectations.

'Someone who's gone as far as you in such a short time is an inspiration.'

'What a speech!'

Sincere compliments are the best. Kind remarks are better than nothing. There's usually something you can find to praise or at the least comment on positively.

Most people who work in the public gaze, from film stars and actors to novelists and celebrity chefs, crave reassurance. Publicity is important to them so they look for a warm reception and silence puts out the wrong vibes. The advice is: if you can say something flattering do; if you can't, then keep quiet – but whatever you do, keep hostile thoughts to yourself. Barry Norman, who worked on the *Daily Mail* for many years, says you start from the understanding that most stars are acutely conscious of thrusting young talent eager to displace them.

They *can* do better

So far, we've been in that happy land where interviewees gladly respond. Their answers may be incomplete or unclear, but under extra questioning they give vivid instances, lively anecdotes and fill out incomplete replies, providing in full the answers you seek. They're neither monosyllabic nor gabby, neither evasive or hostile. Sadly, as everyone discovers, interviewees aren't always like that.

What if your approach has been faultless and your questions good, yet you're disappointed with the quality or amount of information provided? We now shift up a gear to techniques to use on those who give less than you want, don't give, or are evasive or reluctant to answer. These ploys come in no order of efficacy – success depends on skilful use in the right hands on a suitable interviewee. Nor do the techniques come with a guarantee. News management is now so sophisticated that journalists must accept that on occasion they won't win. That doesn't mean capitulate – though it may mean sometimes appear to capitulate. (See pages 121–2; more on news management techniques, pages 68–9 and 105–6; and suggested ways to circumvent reluctance, see the rest of this chapter.) You can choose to:

- persist
- keep them talking
- suggest/guess
- hint at dissatisfaction
- wheedle and needle
- threaten 'no comment'
- float a rumour
- pose a similar but hypothetical situation
- play 'grandmother's footsteps'
- get tough
- tell a story
- offer a confidence.

Persist

If your interviewee doesn't want to answer, you may decide to move on to the next subject. That is tantamount to admitting defeat unless you do so deliberately, intending to return to the subject later. You're there to get the interview, so ask the question again, maybe in a softer or more oblique form, maybe more forcefully. Tell them this is a valuable opportunity to set the record straight, dispel rumours, put their side of the story. Try any ploy you feel comfortable with.

'So the question's too hard for you?' may not suit everyone, but if said jokingly it can ease the tension, which is sometimes all it takes. If they continue to refuse to answer, move on but return and ask it again later.

Keep them talking

Keep your cool, keep your head and keep them talking. The more they talk, the more noticeable refusals are.

I once interviewed a man who insisted on seeing the questions in advance. He was six months into a very difficult and newly created job, had attracted a lot of flak and had previously refused to talk. I faxed over 20 questions, was given an hour and told by his secretary he'd be all right if I could make him laugh.

After the preliminaries, I started on my questions. He refused point blank to answer the first six questions, all about sales and market share. An inauspicious start. I changed tack and we started to talk in general terms, we both relaxed a little and he did start to laugh. By the end of 45 minutes he was chatting away openly and volubly about what a success the company was, so I chanced it: 'C'mon, all's going well, you're surely not going to hide your successes. Just tell me . . .'

And he did. None of the figures was accurate, I am certain – he left not too long after – but 'sourced' they made interesting reading. My belief is that he'd disclosed too much to withdraw at the critical point, realising how damaging it would look. I listened back to that tape a lot and it's possible to hear his voice drop and change tone as he begins to give the highly suspect figures.

Suggest/guess

This is the simplest and often the most effective way of coping with reluctance about statistics.

>'We're spending more than a quarter of a million.'

>'Would that be more than £300,000 or £400,000?'

It depends how practised your interviewees are. If they say 'Yes', then another figure will be suggested.

>'More than half a million?' and so on.

Suppose they reply:

>'We'd rather not discuss the actual budget.'

A comeback could be:

>'Would between £1 and £2 million be a safe bet?'

Again, if they reply 'Yes', you can go on narrowing down until either you get to roughly a printable answer or they pull out. After a second blunt refusal it is best to give up. You can always refer to the refusal to answer in your copy.

There are occasions when a grossly improbable guess may give you a clue how near you are, as people tend to deny wild improbabilities more fervently than close-to-the-mark guesses. Watching body language can help gauge any response.

Hint at dissatisfaction

One way to encourage your interviewee to give more is to get your disappointment across. First, the (slightly more) subtle approach. If you're using a notebook and pen, quietly put the cap back on the pen or close the notebook. A colleague discovered this by chance when interviewing the manager of Pebble Beach Country Club south of San Francisco:

> 'We'd had a very good interview indeed. "How much do you earn?" I asked at one point and he told me – a rare occurrence but always worth trying.
>
> He was a lively talker with some great stories but in effect we'd descended to chit-chat after lunch, so I closed my notebook and had noticed him watching me. A minute or two later he said something so quote-worthy I had to open the book again. The reasoning is simple. I'd been hanging on his words appreciatively – very good for his ego – then had noticeably switched off. He realised he could get more attention and applause, so started to give again.'

The crueller version is to switch off the tape recorder.

When time is short and you can't afford to close your notebook or turn off the tape recorder, then either blame the editor, features editor, yourself or – last resort – them, but in a kindly way:

> 'This isn't working. I'm obviously asking the wrong questions. Can we start again?'

> 'The editor's setting great store by this interview. He'll give me hell if I don't get something meatier. Can we spice it up a little?'

> 'I'd hoped for something sexier. You've always been so quotable before.'

> 'I'd hoped you would give me something stronger.'

> 'I hate to say this, but I think the editor's going to say this is all a little predictable.'

> 'I'm back on writing wedding captions if I don't get some really powerful quote – so *please!*'

Wheedle and needle

Plead or prod – not everyone can or would want to, but it's very effective when practised by a skilled interviewer.

> 'Oh, come on, you can tell me . . .'

> 'Why won't you say? Oh, please . . .'

'You're not too afraid to tell, surely?'

'Question too hard, I guess.'

Threaten 'no comment'

If your interviewee refuses to answer a particular question, one approach is to point out how bad that will look in print. A lot depends on the reputation of your publication. The higher it's rated, the worse an omission looks. This ploy works better on the inexperienced interviewee. Always worth a try.

Float a rumour

This is an insider variation on the 'suggest-an-answer' tactic, requiring the ground to be prepared carefully beforehand. It goes this way. A journalist wants to find out how the fashion chain's business is going after a mammoth expansion but no one will say. He/she asks the chief executive of the chain:

> 'What's this I hear about the downturn in takings in your West Midlands operation?'
> 'What! Where did you hear this?'
> 'On the grapevine.'

If on one or two previous occasions the journalist has presented a real tip this way, the chief executive should have developed a healthy respect for the journalist's sources and – the hope is – should either spill the beans or deny on the record. It does work, I can vouch for that. However, if you overdo it – like so much in journalism – you'll be sussed.

Pose a similar but hypothetical situation

Always worth a try if you're a natural-born wheedler, persistent and/or cheeky, but few people would fall for this one.

Play 'grandmother's footsteps'

This requires great delicacy. Having established what your interviewee does not want to talk about, you creep up to the subject again and again from all angles, veering away at the last minute. They've already signalled that they're unhappy to talk about it and if you're a skilled practitioner you can really rattle them so that in the end – the theory goes – they're relieved to be able to discuss it. This requires confidence and skill (see Andrew Duncan, p. 117).

Get tough

The ground rules of interviewing are to be sceptical not adversarial and never to antagonise interviewees. Break them at your peril. However, with a particularly frustrating interviewee who has resisted every gambit you know and whom you can afford to antagonise, you might consider a hostile question. But ask it with a smile and never lose your temper. If all else fails, insult them – but only if you never need to talk to them again.

Tell a story

An anecdote will tell readers more about a person than any amount of description. To encourage the interviewee to provide one, tell a watered-down version of one in the cuttings which they may be delighted to retell with advantage or offer a new one.

Offer a confidence

This isn't as creepy as it sounds when done unintentionally. Done deliberately it can be tacky.

Interviewer and interviewee, a novelist, are getting along well. Common ground has been established – they've discovered they have both just finished long-term relationships and both are addicted to chocolate.

The novel contains vivid sex scenes and is strong on anxiety and what can be transmitted. The interviewer can't resist saying:

> 'I got thrush once and had to visit an STD clinic. At first I was terrified but ended up quite fancying the consultant.'
> 'That's astonishing,' says the novelist. 'Happened to me too.'

There's a pause. The novelist is asking herself which person's visit to an STD clinic is likely to end up in print.

Questions *not* to ask

- Don't prove how stupid you are by asking smart-ass, clever-clever questions. They infuriate interviewees (a) because you're showing off rather than trying to gather information and (b) because it breaks the important 'they're-the-star' guideline.
- Don't ask the first question that leaps to mind. It will have leapt to every other mind, too.
- Don't badger or hector. It's counter-productive.

- Don't ask what you should have known from research.
- Above all, don't ask: 'How do you feel?'

> 'Your mother's been eaten by a crocodile, your father's been
> electrocuted and your husband's gone missing in Borneo.
> How do you feel?'

People who want to tell you how they feel won't need this question to prompt them, and people who can't put feelings into words won't need it either.

Ploys *not* to fall for

Beware if you're asked for your opinion. This is an experienced interviewee's way of flattering you, getting you on their side and so stopping probing assessments. The interviewee is turning the tables: using a successful interviewing ploy on you. See p. 136.

'Tell me about you . . .' Shrewd, manipulative or very nice interviewees may ask you questions about yourself. Deflect these immediately.

Lynn Barber recounts how Julie Andrews asked at one point if Lynn had any children. She has two daughters but said she had none, because she knew Julie Andrews, being a pleasant woman, would ask about them and she didn't want to divert or break the flow of the interview. (Lynda Lee-Potter's approach, p. 129.)

5
Understanding interviewees and avoiding problems

We speak with our voices but communicate with our whole bodies. Not an original idea but one often dismissed by word-oriented journalists. Trainers, who watch a lot of interviews, become body language converts. They observe an aggressive posture adopted by the interviewer and see how it puts an interviewee on the defensive. They recognise from a cluster of movements that the question just asked has hit a target that the interviewee is unwilling to discuss.

Interviewees, primarily concerned with their responses, know how they felt about the question or the interviewer. Often after watching a recording of the interview they understand how the question or the questioner's body language affected them, or see how their body language showed what they were feeling.

Journalists – particularly beginners – are much harder to convince, probably because they're tuned to what's said and getting that down accurately, so much so that at first they are deaf to the subtleties of body language.

Body language is not an *exact* science. Folded arms may mean that interviewees feel defensive or that they sit that way because they find it comfortable. Shifts in posture become significant and worth noting when an interviewee who has been leaning forward and talking freely, suddenly leans back and folds their arms. Something caused the change, most likely what was being talked about at that time. That *is* worth following up.

The most important aspects for interviewers are:

- appearance
- eyes
- face
- gestures
- head
- posture.

Appearance

This conveys the most immediate impression but also is the one that can most easily be changed. Chewed fingernails can be covered with false ones. Expensive accessories such as a Fendi handbag can add lustre to, though not totally disguise, a Marks & Sparks trouser suit. An expensive haircut can transform a person.

Though appearance makes an immediate impact, a warm engaging character soon means that weird clothes, down-at-heel shoes or chewed fingernails move down the ratings ladder. As one ugly charmer said: 'Give me five minutes and they'll forget the face.'

That aside, what interviewees wear tells you something, from Popeye ties to Bill Gates's famously grubby glasses. Beards and spectacles are often used as protection, as distancing. It's well known that overweight men with beards often shave them off once they have shed a lot of weight. A chairman of British Aerospace told a *Financial Times* reporter that he wore a beard because it saved him 10 minutes a day shaving time, which built to an hour a week, five whole days a year.

Fraud investigator Mike Comer, chief executive of the international company Maxima, says he looks for inconsistencies: 'A reasonably average suit with perhaps a gold Rolex watch.' He's particularly suspicious of men with fancy shoes – crocodile skin, buckles, tassels, silk socks. 'I think most of the crooks I've dealt with have had some hang-up with their feet.'

Eyes

You must look at the person you're interviewing, the only exceptions being when you're making notes, checking your questions or perhaps encouraging confessions (see p. 139). Don't drop your eyes when your interviewee looks at you. This is a signal you are not enjoying their company, but don't read the same into their eye movements. People look away while talking, particularly if recalling incidents and anecdotes. However, people who talk to you with their eyes closed may either be bored or feel superior; either way they don't feel like eyeballing you.

Continued eye contact while listening indicates approval, encouragement and positive feedback. The more people look at each other, the more they grow to like each other. It's staring that makes people uncomfortable, since starers are seen as dominant.

Once you are confident about meeting interviewees, you might start to look which way the interviewee's eyes flick when they break after first contact. This could give some indication whether they tend to be artistic and have good visual imaginations (break to their left) or scientific (right).

You can test this yourself with a colleague. Sit so that you can observe their eye movements clearly and ask them to think about their bedroom when they were eight. Odds are that they will look up and to their left. Ask them what features they'd most like in a new kitchen, and odds are they will look up to the right. Ask them to remember what was the last thing said to them at work the previous day, and odds are they will look to their left. Ask them to think what they'd like to say if they had two minutes on TV and they may look to their right.

Ask them to think about the rules of football and they may well look down to their left. Ask about their feelings on capital punishment, and they may well look down to the right. The theory is that people look upwards when recalling or constructing images; on the level when they're remembering what's been said or trying to put things into words; and downwards when recalling feelings or having an internal dialogue.

All this may be of no use to you in any interview, but you never know. Some investigative journalists certainly use it as an indicator of whether an actual (truthful) location or image is being remembered (up and left) or an invented one (up and right).

Lying is covered on p. 63. Here it's enough to say that if an interviewee's eyes flick quickly away before answering a key question, ask it then or later in another way and watch their body language very carefully.

Finally, attractive, expressive eyes are a very useful asset to interviewers of both sexes.

Face

People's faces can register all sorts of emotion – fear, happiness, misery, anger, surprise, contempt – but rarely during an interview, as most people learn to control their expressions.

Experienced interviewees, business people particularly, are good at this, though occasionally the mask slips and there's a fleeting glimpse of anger at a particularly annoying question. The skill is to watch for changes of expression – maybe from interested listening to a cold smile. Why? Or from a real smile to tightened lips and jaw. Again, why?

Observant interviewers have found describing smiles a telling way of indicating character: from the slow, lazy, glinting smile 'like a king crocodile' of the late financial entrepreneur James Goldsmith to the unusual flat, horizontal smile of Kelsey Grammer, star of *Frasier*.

Gestures

Hand signals have a bewildering variety of meanings. For interviewers there are a number of hand 'signals' that merit a mention:

- Steepling, where the hands are in a prayer-like position with fingertips together but palms apart, is said to show seniority, superiority, confidence.
- Index-finger wagging often reveals a bullying, 'I know best' temperament. Some interpreters say the finger represents a Neanderthal club.
- Ticking off points on the fingers of one hand with the forefinger of another, 'One, two, three . . .' is said to show, and probably does, an authoritarian nature.
- Twirling a pair of spectacles round and round mimics the TV 'wind-up-soon' hand signal – and means the same in my experience.
- Pushing real or imaginary items away with the hands and picking or flicking imaginary fluff off clothes is often interpreted as dismissing or rejecting what is being heard, be it question or suggestion.
- A hand near the mouth is often interpreted as a pale echo of the hand involuntarily clapped over the mouth after some appalling indiscretion, suggesting anxiety or even deception. The same is sometimes said of hands near the nose and eyes.
- There's not much agreement about the significance of anything put into the mouth: some say it's for reassurance, some say it masks aggression.
- Hands near the chin are said to show thought.
- Rubbing the back of the neck is read as a sign of frustration – dealing with something or someone that's 'a pain in the neck'.

The position of palms when hands are extended in a conversation can be telling. If an interviewee is trying to explain something to you and says: 'Look . . .' extending a hand, palm up, towards you, it's likely they are more affable than if the hand is extended palm down. Try it out yourself. Palms up equals acceptance; palms down negation.

Hand movements can provide the hand-mover with reassurance. Neck-stroking, mouth-touching movements are called 'pacifiers'. Interviewees suddenly exhibiting these may be trying to calm themselves down.

Arms can be used as a defence (crossed), to welcome (open) or to attack (thrust out). Legs can be uncrossed, splayed or crossed in a variety of ways, and much here depends on conditioning. Tightly crossed legs, legs crossed 'in parallel' or crossed legs tucked securely under a chair are usually all signs of nervousness, insecurity, withdrawal or lack of co-operation in both sexes.

Men who sit legs wide apart are said to be 'displaying', sending out a sexual message. If they sit with one foot resting on the other knee, the 'figure four' position, this is interpreted as being relaxed and open. It's more common in North America than Europe. It's impossible to generalise with women: some are trained to cross their ankles but never their legs, others never to sit cross-legged at all. Most do what's comfortable.

The important thing about the crossing and uncrossing of legs is when it occurs. It happens for a number of reasons, obviously, but particularly when interviewees feel uncomfortable. You've only got to do a few interviews to realise the truth of this. The skilled interviewer needs to notice if this occurs at any significant point in the questioning.

At one smart press conference about corporate sponsorship, four captains of industry sat on a raised platform without the benefit of desk or table to shield them. The questioning was going well until one journalist asked: 'What of the supposed influence of the chairman's wife in deciding what to sponsor?' Four pairs of legs uncrossed and recrossed simultaneously. It made me realise why so many politicians feel happier behind a desk or table.

Feet are the greatest giveaways. Just as 21st-century man still experiences a surge of adrenalin in a tight corner – the fight or flight response of primitive man – so the feet of 21st-century interviewees still begin to shuffle or shift when they want to get away.

Feet are the hardest part of the body to control. If they suddenly start to tap or twitch, the interviewee isn't comfortable. If an interviewee turns and points their feet towards the exit, that small movement may express a subconscious desire to leave.

Head

Nods and head tilts signal encouragement and approval, so they're much more useful to the interviewer than the interviewee. What matters about the interviewee's head movements is how the head is carried: forward of the body looks rather aggressive; high generally gives an impression of superiority; dropped usually suggests depression or submission.

Posture

In a straightforward, uncomplicated interview, an interviewee leaning forward or towards you shows that everything is going well. You have engaged their interest and attention. If they are leaning away or backwards, they may either be very relaxed or have switched off and lost interest.

Leaning forward symmetrically, with both arms on the desk or table top, is said to indicate a more involved attitude than the asymmetrical lean – one arm resting on the arm of a chair, or the desk – which is said to show relaxation.

An interviewee's posture becomes harder to read in more complex interviews. They may be leaning away because you have just touched on something they do not wish to discuss.

Receive *and* send

One of the pluses of becoming proficient in reading body language is the realisation that you can use it to communicate with interviewees.

- Lean towards the interviewee and they'll talk more, sensing that you like them.
- Nod and they'll carry on talking up to three or four times longer than otherwise. By contrast, refusing to nod can make an interviewee dry up.
- You want to interrupt? Lean forward and raise your head and your hand slightly. Or try three nods, that can work, too.
- They're talking too much? Cut back on the nods, lean back, look away and sigh softly or adopt a posture that is totally contradictory to theirs.
- You suspect they're telling porkies? Cover your mouth and flick imaginary fluff from your jacket. If you catch their eye, look away for a second.

Because you get back very much what you send, it's important to sit comfortably, avoiding legs tightly twisted, crossed or clamped together. Badly done, attempts at control through body language will disturb your interviewee consciously or subconsciously. So practise first and be subtle.

Poker face

When John Lennon told Maureen Cleave that the Beatles were more famous than Jesus Christ you can bet she *didn't* say 'Wow! You really mean that? You can't be that big-headed!' No, it's a fair bet she nodded and listened, then asked another question. When the story was printed it caused a furore.

The moral: don't let on if you're given a great quote – if you do, your interviewee may twig and backtrack or clam up, neither of which you want.

Lying

It's a trusting and naive journalist who thinks they are never lied to. The lies may be minor – the result of interviewees wanting to present themselves in a favourable light or because they want to fool the neighbours. They may even believe what they say at the time.

On occasion, though, the lies are serious and designed to mislead: to bolster a company's share price, for example, or avoid prosecution. Sometimes lying is inevitable because it's necessary: cabinet reshuffles, for example, budget plans, company failures. Sometimes the lie is to protect reputations – the liar's or someone else's.

Sometimes the interviewee has forgotten the truth. It's established that the more you tell a lie, the more you accept it as the truth until in the end you believe it. Sometimes the interviewee is passing on what they've been told, believing that to be true.

How journalists react when they suspect they're being lied to depends on who they're interviewing and writing for. With some interviewees you can laugh and say 'Come off it, that can't be true . . .' With others, raise an eyebrow or smile mockingly. With others, nod sagely while remaining sceptical and return to query the statement later in the interview. Or you can appear deeply impressed but store it away for a later occasion. It's a judgment that only the interviewer can make.

Whatever the reason, lying matters – particularly in interviewing for news and business stories. If someone lies, there's usually a story there.

It is very hard for most people to keep their eye movements under control when lying. People who have gazed steadily at you for the first 20 minutes of the interview may, quite involuntarily, blink more or glance away for a fraction of a second before telling a lie. But there's no one sure way to tell. For a start, good liars practise. Remember Oliver North and Contragate/Irangate? He stood up straight, raised his right hand, looked unswervingly ahead and swore to tell the truth, the whole truth and nothing but the truth, so help him God. Then he lied.

Good liars look you straight in the eye and speak up boldly with no hesitation or telltale lowering or raising of the voice. Jonathan Aitken practised lying and developed it very successfully until brought down by a combination of *Guardian* journalists, Mohammed al-Fayed and his own pride.

Clues

Some verbal and vocal clues to evasion or avoidance of the truth are easily recognisable but others require great concentration from journalists using shorthand, though they can be studied at leisure on tapes.

Easily recognisable clues include an immediate reluctance to answer, in full, in part or in any detail. For example, 'I can't tell you that . . . That's all I know . . .' It's always safer for someone avoiding the truth to say 'I can't remember' than to provide any detail. Be more inclined to accept a 'Can't remember' explanation if there's a pause before it's said, while the interviewee genuinely tries to recall.

Should the interviewer challenge a 'Can't remember' answer, the interviewee may play for time by asking for clarification, countering with a question, answering a question which hasn't been asked, with contrived anger, extreme politeness, flattery, long rambling answers or emphatic repetition, 'Yes, yes, yes . . .' 'No, no, no. . . .'

Amateurs are the easiest to suss and even then the indications are not foolproof but there are guidelines to help. Maxima, the London-based company specialising in fraud detection world-wide, have developed a checklist of visual, verbal and vocal clues that indicate interviewees may be lying, but they emphasise there is no single response that can be judged conclusive. The checklist has been devised after studying interviews designed specifically to establish the truth where, for example, evidence may be produced or previous answers questioned. Even so, it's valuable for investigative and business journalists.

Maxima estimate that managers are lied to on average about 30 times each week. An important distinction is made between good and bad lies; good being the 'like your hat' or 'wonderful meal' type of comment. Maxima's chief executive, Mike Comer, believes that the chances of most people detecting lies are no better than 50:50. On average, he reports, police officers and psychiatrists score only slightly better. Interestingly, the most effective group at detecting deceit were a group of criminals serving life sentences.

Comer says that it is possible for experienced interviewers, using a mixture of techniques, to achieve a much higher success rate if interviewees are judged on:

- the words they use and how they use them
- their attitude
- the emotions they display
- their body language.

He places great reliance on both spoken and body language, for example:

- quiet replies, when previously the interviewee has been speaking more loudly
- noticeably slower replies then given previously.

Posture

Comer believes posture is one of the most reliable visual giveaways. 'What you are looking for are significant changes in posture at times of significant questions.' These can be turning or leaning away from the interviewer, pushing the chair further back, getting up from a chair, or pushing away with the hands.

'People seldom lie to you "head on",' he says. 'They almost always sit at an oblique angle.' Any increased use of 'pacifier' hand movements he sees as a subconscious reaction to feeling uncomfortable and he says that if someone who has been using a lot of hand movements to accompany what they're saying suddenly – at a key point in the interview – clasps their hands together, puts them in their pockets or behind their head, that's probably a good indication they're hiding something.

Memory

Part of his guidance rests on the fact that recalling truth depends on memory, which is detailed, easy to retrieve and can usually be repeated with confidence. By contrast, deception is based on imagination, and has to be constructed and remembered each time.

To quote Maxima's excellent guide 'Finding the Truth . . .', 'Memory can be considered similar to a read-only, fast, random access computer chip or hard disk. It can be accessed quickly and in any order. Imagination is akin to a read-and-write, sequentially accessed tape drive which is slow and difficult to access.' That's why Maxima believe that pauses before delivery are one indicator of lying.

Foot movements are another. 'The further you are from the face, the nearer you are to the truth,' says one body language expert. They can also show boredom. Context determines which of the two it is.

AVOIDING PROBLEMS

Because interviewing is so complex, a lot can go wrong. Patently it's unwise to wear a 'Woman's Right to Choose' tee-shirt when interviewing a pro-Lifer. But who's to know that your interviewee has a pathological distrust of people who wear lime green, or detests the name Marcus, or loathes a Liverpool accent?

Avoiding action

First, recognise you're not going to get it right every time. You're bound to make mistakes, but practice does bring progress.

Aim to go into every interview as well prepared as possible. Recognise that many if not most of the people you interview early in your career will be well practised and skilled at getting their message across. You may come away thinking things went well when actually you've been neatly manoeuvred into writing at their behest. This is why planning is so important, why 'Know what you want to know' is one of the earliest injunctions. It's your best protection against being a sacrificial lamb, going all unknowing to the slaughter.

Many problems can be minimised by following some simple guidelines:

- Don't be in a hurry. It's insulting and demeans your interviewee's contribution. By all means tell them what time you have available, but during the interview don't rush or push them in any way. If you have to look at a watch, be sure it's theirs – *never* yours. When you go, be full of regrets.
- Don't talk about yourself. This antagonises. They are the star of the interview. You are there to gather their thoughts, not contribute yours. The only time you should talk about yourself is in the very early rapport-building stage.
- Don't offer your own negative judgments. Would you talk to the person who is to write the story if they rubbish your contribution?
- Don't ask long, convoluted questions.

It's also within your power to ensure you:

- don't make a poor impression when you walk through the door;
- don't arrive under-prepared and easy to fool;
- don't get behind in note-taking and miss a great quote;
- don't alienate them by an injudicious remark;
- don't let them take control;
- don't miss vital clues.

WHAT CAN GO WRONG

Let's start with the most important.

You can let them take control

Dangerous. You are told only what they want you to know, not what you want to find out. You might as well print a press release verbatim. Don't despair if it happens to you, just ensure it doesn't happen again. 'Catch me once, shame on you. Catch me twice, shame on me.'

If as a beginner you're caught this way, it will be because you're up against a well-trained interviewee, and the first thing they've been taught is to get down on their knees and thank God for a poorly prepared journalist. 'From a corporate view, journalists who ask vague questions are actually a huge advantage,' says Monica Esslin, managing director of Phoenix Associates International. She trains executives from transnationals such as Philips and Compaq. 'It means the executive can grab the agenda and say what they want to say.'

No worries

Esslin educates executives in the ways of the press. They are taught not to be wary because in the past they've been misquoted; instead to pre-empt this by arriving with their own agenda and ensuring they get their message across. 'We teach interviewees to take control – and then they don't need to worry.'

Esslin spends considerable time enlightening her clients about the woolly heads of inept interviewers. 'They're not going to search through 30 minutes of a tape looking for important messages,' she says. 'You have to get your message across in the first three answers.' She trains clients who regularly do eight half-hour face-to-face interviews in the afternoon with journalists who have sat through a presentation in the morning. They are taught to recognise the poor mutt who has lost the press release, hasn't read the press release or else has read it but has already forgotten what it says.

> 'What staggers me is how many journalists waste so much time wading back through the press release – proof that they're not thinking. With a good press release and a good press pack, journalists should be framing the story in their head and, when they get to interview the relevant executive, should need around three or four quotes for the story – about five to ten minutes – then the rest of the time you can get info for your next feature, sort out a facility visit, develop the relationship further.'

The worst sin in Esslin's eyes? Wasting time going through company history when it's all on their web site.

Esslin-trained executives are taught to 'word-bridge' or 'loop'. They learn that it doesn't matter what people ask because they don't treat the question as something that has to be answered literally.

> 'The question is an indication of a topic or area or belief or thought behind that question that you might choose to talk about. You can't do this unless you can create a bridge between something in the question and what you want to talk about. You're always going to bridge away from what you don't want to talk about.'

Counter-ploys

What do journalists need to counter all this training? 'Every weapon in the armoury,' says Esslin. First, training to understand what makes a story, the wit to work out what angle you're after, what information you need.

She rates honesty, too. 'Every time you admit you don't understand something you win a thousand brownie points from the person you are interviewing,' she says. 'Most are more than willing to help you. What doesn't help is going nod, nod, nod, yes of course, when you don't understand.'

She also rates curiosity and believes this draws out better responses than clever-clever questions designed to impress. Because she trained as a journalist, she admires skilled interviewers who know how to establish rapport, build trust and cope with bridging. Faced with these interviewers, Esslin-trained interviewees are on their guard. 'We warn them not to relax.'

The journalists she admires arrive knowing what they want to know and are able to keep four story lines in their head, asking questions about each angle, mixing them up. This can puzzle or confuse an interviewee, which is very useful from the journalist's point of view because it deflects the interviewee from their pre-set agenda.

All good interviewers use the 'loop and circle' counter-ploy, neatly returning to points they want clarified, questions they want answered. Well done, it accumulates evidence, stacking up 'proof points' and slowly closes the net around the story.

Among the more complex weapons in a journalist's armoury, Esslin rates body language and linguistic patterns. 'Influencing techniques, used covertly or overtly, take quite a bit of learning but they absolutely do work.' Matching posture is the technique Esslin rates highest. She also believes in linguistic pattern mirroring. The idea is that if someone says 'I see what you mean', the interviewer talks to them using visual words, but if they say 'I believe', the interviewer uses cognitive language. For more techniques used by clever interviewees against journalists, see pages 105–6 and 135–6.

Esslin ends with a chilling thought. 'There are whole chunks of journalism effectively run by PR companies.'

You can alienate them

Make injudicious comments on what you're told and you could be in real trouble.

> 'I went to Sarum Hill Academy but left last year.'
> 'Not surprised. It's an absolute dump my friends tell me. Deadhead tutors. Is Jim Ilett – the one they call 'Boredom Personified Ilett' – still there?'
> 'Yes. Actually he's my uncle.'

> 'So when I was fired, to cheer myself up I went to see *Police Academy* and it really worked.'

'Yeah – great film! Didn't you love the Commandant's speech?'
'To be honest, I loathed it: puerile and disgusting. Walked out halfway through and bumped into an old friend who told me about a job going at ITN.'

'I have to go to North Wales tonight but I'm not looking forward to it.'
'Yeah – nice country, shame about the people.'
'I'm going to my grandmother's funeral.'

You can bore them

You've got to make interviews interesting for your interviewee. Sometimes you'll be the twelfth person who's interviewed them that day. They'll be on auto-pilot and will wearily produce well-rehearsed answers unless you break the cycle with a fresh approach.

Probably the best way is to commiserate, to share the suffering: after all, you're both in a poor position. They're exhausted and you've drawn the short straw by going last. Use it to your advantage. By drawing attention to it, you show yourself in a sympathetic light, not just the last in a long line of bloodsuckers, asking the same question, and so you put them on their metal.

Give your questions a fresh twist and see if they can give you a fresh angle. You could even suggest opening the windows for some fresh air, or doing the interview walking round the block. Anything to break the monotony.

You can mishear

In an interview with best-selling authors for *TV Times*, one journalist misheard 'bodice ripper' as 'body stripper'. A local paper had to apologise: 'We are sorry we said the baby was found on a rubbish heap. This should have read "a rubber sheet".'

The *Guardian* quoted Bono of U2 as saying 'I became a fan of club music, of *drug culture*, of everything that was going on at the time' – later correcting it to 'I became a fan of club music, of *club culture* . . .'.

Another *Guardian* correction:

> In our lead feature . . . about cannabis, we asked people whether they smoked it and quoted the former leader of the SNP, Alex Salmond, as saying: 'If you say "yes", people claim you're encouraging and supporting it and if you say "no", it looks like you're a prick.' Mr Salmond has asked us to make it clear that what he actually said was 'prig' not 'prick'.

The moral is obvious. If the quote sounds at all unusual, or you're not sure you've heard correctly, query it, and never presume your interviewee uses the same language that you do.

You can misunderstand

Easily done. Your protection is total concentration, excellent research and a brain that hears, assesses and cross-checks information for consistency and sense.

> 'I've never been to Spain. The furthest south I've been is Parma.'
> 'But Palma's in Majorca, surely?'
> 'No, no. Parma in Italy, where the ham comes from. P a r m a.'

You can lose the thread

You may feel it makes you look stupid to admit you don't understand what's being said, but you'll look far more stupid if you get it wrong in print.

You can show your hand

If you have an agenda you'd rather they didn't know about, don't make it clear from the very start by the thrust of your questions. Most political and business interviewees have considerable experience of the press, more than beginners realise, and subtlety is needed.

HOW TO COPE WITH DIFFICULT INTERVIEWEES

What do you do when the trouble comes from your interviewees? How do you cope with the waffly, the evasive, the hostile and the monosyllabic? With charm, of course. With delicacy. And with deft firmness: with the waffly and the evasive you take control, not by wrenching it back but by using the velvet choke chain operated by the iron hand. With the hostile and the monosyllabic you flip roles, slow down, vary your questions dramatically, become a shape-shifter, a changeling, a will-o'-the-wisp.

The wafflers

They may be nervous prattlers spewing out rubbish or they may be egomaniacs in love with their opinions. Either way they talk too much and over-answer the question, adding, revising, rambling, diverging, sub-clausing, reminiscing

. . . Stop! Rein them in. As always, honesty works best – but honesty of a subtle tint.

> 'What you say is amazing. I could listen all day but I have to move us on. What about . . .'

The honesty here is partial but undeniable. Their waffle powers *are* amazing and you *could* listen all day – though you'd rather not. Note the 'move us on', kinder than 'move you on'. Go gently to the next question. If you're too brutal they will most likely clam up. They usually know they talk a lot, because friends will have told them.

Use all the body language devices to interrupt, of course. (See p. 63.)

The evaders

More a velvet harness needed than a choke chain, here. Evaders slide off the subject with ease. One sentence they're appearing to answer the question about enforcing the speed limit and the next they're talking about how effective traffic calming measures can be and how cheap they are to install and wow, you're off on to budgets.

A discussion about a big high street multiple's disappointing sales somehow turns into a conversation about the latest street fashions. Or questions about difficulties with software prompt details of an amazing new computer add-on. You've been 'looped' or 'word-bridged'. You should loop or word-bridge back.

> 'Fascinating, but what I really want to know is . . .'

> 'Wow, really – but first let's get back to . . .'

> 'That's a great story. I'd like to know much more – but first I'd like to clear up . . .'

Said smiling, and done with charm, this is a clear message that they've been sussed.

The hostile

These are the bullies, the aggressive bastards who power their way through regardless. Ask them a question they don't welcome and they go straight on the attack. What they expect in return is aggression or submission.

Aggression they can cope with because that's their speciality. They'll win here. Submission suits them fine, too. What they don't expect is amused surprise, a calm level gaze, a longish pause, concern for their blood pressure, a delighted 'that certainly hit home' or a tut-tutting 'dear me, we are upset . . . What *is* the matter?'

You must never be angry or hostile in return. If you lose your temper you lose the encounter. You have to force a change of pace, of tone, of approach. You can stand your ground, adult to adult, and ask the question again. This is the assertive route.

> 'What you just said in my opinion didn't answer the question. So I'll ask it again . . .'

You can try assertiveness plus a dig:

> 'What you just said in my opinion didn't answer the question. So I'll ask it again and hope this time you'll provide a more useful/more relevant/less hostile answer . . .'

You should be able to flip out of your initial role of uncomplicated interviewer into an assortment of others, all designed to assert your control of yourself and the interview. You could become a concerned comrade:

> 'It's not a good idea to get so riled. You'd best be careful or you might damage your health.'

You could try a put-down or two. Annoying a hostile interviewee pays off because you win in two ways: they lose their temper and lose control.

> 'So who's got their knickers in a twist now? And all I asked was . . .'

Or if they're old (say over 45):

> 'Keep your hair on!'

If they're not someone you have to interview regularly and you can afford really to annoy them, laugh at them. This will make you no friends but may provoke some good quotes. Power hates being mocked.

The monosyllabic

A nightmare, a challenge, the pits – the worst interviewees of all. They 'yes' or 'no' wherever they can and answer 'Can't say' or 'Don't know' far too often. On the basis that they have agreed to be interviewed and so have something to gain from the exchange, the charitable approach is that they're tongue-tied, reticent, shy, upset, slow thinkers. They may well be any or all of those, though sometimes they're just bloody, in a filthy temper, fed up or want to be rid of you.

The tactics are two-fold. The first is to ease down, to talk more slowly and pause at least four or five seconds before asking the next question. Really pause and look keen to learn the answer. Listen carefully without being too intense.

The second tactic is to ask precise questions that call for long detailed answers. A flood victim with three ceilings down when asked 'What was it like?' replies 'Horrible'. Asked 'What did you do?' replies 'Panicked!' Asked, 'What happened?' replies: 'A pipe burst'.

The same flood victim, if asked: 'Talk me through how you discovered the flood,' might reply:

> 'I'd been away for the weekend and came back to find water running down the hall. I went into the drawing room and water was dripping down the candelabra.
>
> I went upstairs to find the ceiling down and the room open to the loft, with the sky showing through. I had rockwool insulation in the loft and there was plaster and filthy rockwool everywhere, splattered up the walls, over the furniture. I panicked and ran round saying, "Oh my God, oh my God." Then I got a grip on myself and thought, "You'd better turn the water off." So I went down into the basement – which of course was flooded – and turned it off. After a while the dripping stopped and by that time something worse has occurred to me: had I paid my insurance?
>
> I dug it out and found I had, mercifully. There was a number to call and I called it. Within two hours three strong men had arrived and started heaving sodden carpets and rugs out and moving ruined sofas. They left a pump working in the basement and set up three de-humidifiers.'

The questions to ask are the ones that call for descriptive answers – *Where? What? When?*

> 'Tell me all about . . .'
>
> 'Talk me through exactly what happened . . .'
>
> 'Describe your day to me . . .'

Phrasing these questions takes practice but is worth all the effort in coaxing replies from this most challenging category of interviewees.

A last thought from Lynn Barber on interviewing bores: 'I found the only way was to ask completely batty questions, to try and startle them into saying something fresh.'

6
Checking and editing quotes

You're out the door, having thanked your interviewee, packed away your note-book or tape recorder, collected your belongings and checked that if for any reason you have to get back, your interviewee has no objection and you know where they'll be.

If you have been taping the interview, the number one priority now is to listen back to the end of the cassette to ensure you have the interview safely recorded. If you checked voice levels at the very beginning and kept an eye on the recorder there should be no problem, but accidents do happen.

Linda Kelsey, when editor of *Cosmopolitan*, didn't discover till she asked her secretary to type back the tape of her interview with Bob Geldof that the batteries had failed after the first 10 minutes. If this should happen, you must do an immediate brain dump: write down every single thing you can remember about the interview. Don't panic – take several deep breaths and start by picturing yourself walking into the room to meet the interviewee; closing your eyes can help.

Write down your immediate impressions, what your interviewee was wearing, what the room looked like. Go back to what you said and their response. Look again at your list of questions and try to hear the replies in your mind's ear. Write down everything. You'll be amazed how much you can remember. Though you can phone back later to check on missing facts or check spellings, remember that a repeat interview is never as successful.

Journalists using shorthand are protected from this disaster. Their equivalent is the lost notebook, so always keep it close. If you're driving back from an interview, don't leave it in a briefcase in the car while you pay for petrol or have a cup of tea. Bags get snatched and cars get stolen. For the same reason, if you're on a press trip abroad don't pack your notebook, photographs or any background material in luggage that goes in the hold or leave them in a car or coach overnight.

Consider this horror story: after spending much of Friday interviewing a prickly interviewee and being lent some treasured drawings, the journalist is met off the train by her sister. She throws her notebooks and the drawings into the back of the car and off they go for a meal with friends, where they change, then go out clubbing.

> 'We came out of the club at 6 in the morning. The car had been broken into. Everything had gone. Everything. My notes, the drawings, everything – and you know you can never recreate the freshness of an interview. We went home in total shock, went to bed and woke up to hear the phone ringing. Some woman in south London had found everything including my Filofax. She'd looked under M for mother and had rung her.
>
> We went round to the woman's house and found bits of paper hanging up to dry all over the place. The whole lot had been dumped in a puddle. I work with ink and the notes looked like water-colour drawings. I could see the odd word here and there and luckily I can usually get it back if I transcribe my notes early enough. It was a nightmare. Luckily the drawings were in a plastic bag.'

Interviewers with shorthand safely in the notebook, and those reassured that the recorder worked, can now make extra notes of everything significant that was said in the 'twilight zone' after the apparent end of the interview, when the notebook was put away or the recorder turned off. These are often the most revealing comments of all and, provided these notes are made immediately after an interview, are acceptable in court.

Interviewers with a notebook who are going back to the office by train, bus, tube or taxi should grab the first opportunity to read back their notes and scribble down any extra details. It's idiotic not to read back notes the same day you do the interview. We've all made this mistake. Once.

If you can't read your notes, ring the offending words or sections and write down the letters/sounds you can read, leaving gaps to be filled. Rather than beat your brains, leave the problem outlines for a day or two and you may be surprised how easily the sense leaps out at you from the page when you read the notes a second time.

If you're listening back to a fuzzy tape with loads of background noise, play it over again and again, with the bass turned to its lowest setting and the treble to its highest.

Organisation

Because they are insecure, beginners take too many notes but most quickly learn to select what they write down, in effect editing while they listen. This process is speeded by weary hours spent typing back wodges of interviews which are never used. As a result of critically appraising what gets into print, you learn fast what interests readers.

If a story is required immediately, it should be written direct from the notes. If the deadline is delayed, say for a week or two, then it's best to type back all your notes, though tapes needn't – shouldn't – be typed back in their entirety. The most effective method is to listen to the tape on a mains recorder fitted with a counter and to make a note of the numbers where the best quotes or most useful info is, and then type back those sections. Print-outs should be kept in the feature file.

If you find gaps in the interview, facts or perhaps quotes that you feel you should check with your interviewee, then go back as soon as possible. Provided you have 'left the door open' there should be no problem. If you neglected that you'll probably experience a mixture of exasperation (theirs) and embarrassment (yours).

Now is also the time to file away business cards and to update your contacts book or organiser with names, addresses, telephone numbers, email addresses, perhaps the names of your interviewee's partner/children/secretary.

What's missing?

After you've typed back your notes, read them again more analytically. What gaps are there? How best to fill them? What questions remain unanswered? Who might be able to help?

You must also consider how what you've learnt might play in print. Is it libellous? Does anyone named need to be accorded the right of reply? Should you check with a third party to ensure that the story stands up?

If you didn't do so earlier, you should now assess what you've been told during the interview against what you discovered when researching. Are there any discrepancies? Do the statistics and the chronology agree? What follow-ups are needed? Think particularly hard about areas where your interviewee appeared reluctant to talk. Ask yourself what is being covered up.

For example, during apartheid, a South African wine producer took a large group of British journalists to the Beaujolais region to launch its latest venture, a South African equivalent of a beaujolais nouveau – this year's white wine but, since from the southern hemisphere, delivered in the spring.

The group was mixed: wine writers and drinks business writers. It was a lavish trip: private jets, the transformation of a Beaujolais village into a South African wine area. No press conference, just company executives talking to journalists over lavish meals and loads of drink.

The company was talkative about its very good wines but silent about its UK business – how many cases it sold a year. Because of apartheid, some UK customers were then boycotting South African wine, so instead of case sales a company spokesman opted for the percentage route: 'Our UK sales represent x% of total sales'. Requests for details of total sales were met with a blanket refusal.

Because I worked on a monthly I had the time to fax the company in South Africa for its latest annual report and from that was able to work out how many cases were sold in the UK. It was pitifully small. Phoning the London office to check my figures, I was embarrassed to be pleaded with not to print my findings.

Checking

Never knowingly to print anything false, always to strive to be accurate – it sounds moralistic but is the basis on which respect and reputations are built. In the United States, as Ian Katz of the *Guardian* discovered while on secondment to the Washington *Post*, 'the pressure is less to get something into the paper than to get it exactly right'. He recounts how his first piece for the paper's style section finally appeared two weeks after he thought he had finished it, after daily discussions with an editor who wanted hazy details checked, extra quotes, and who added detailed structural and stylistic requests.

> 'I would like to round off the story by reporting that the finished product was not markedly better than my first offering, that it had been robbed of some of its immediacy, even. What a ringing endorsement that would be for the British way of doing things. But it was better, immeasurably so. And in the two (pretty miserable) weeks of editing, I probably learnt more than I had in a year of British journalism.'

He has just one qualifier, relating to the *Post*'s virtual monopoly. 'It is hard to imagine editors being quite as fastidious if four broadsheet competitors were dropping on the back bench every night.'

Never misreport or, if there are gaps in your notes, guess – or your editor might be the recipient of a letter as damaging and astringent as this from Jeremy Paxman to the editor of the *Financial Times*.

> Sir,
> The writer responsible for 'Of monsters and lesser mortals' [a report of a meal with the journalist and author Robert Harris] seems to have learned his trade at the hands of Jeffrey Archer . . .
> It is a pity your correspondent cannot tell the difference between a Gothic Victorian vicarage standing in under one acre of garden and an 18th century pile 'sitting on huge swathes of land in Berkshire'. In the

drawing room of this mansion he alleges that 'Tony – Britain's prime minister to you and me' – unwinds from the stresses and strains of Downing Street. This will certainly be news to 'Tony' as he has never crossed the threshold.

Your correspondent alleges Robert rolled a Cuban cigar 'between his manicured fingers'. Robert is certainly a stranger to the thrills of DIY. But if his hands have ever been buffed and polished by a manicurist, I will personally service his Jaguar.

Your correspondent finally goes on to relate how he 'spluttered' into his '£15 goblet of brandy' at the size of the bill. I really cannot fathom his discomfort, since, when given the choice by Robert of whether they would eat at the local pub or Albert Speer's expensive eatery, your correspondent opted for the latter, with the words: 'The *FT* will pay'.

(*Financial Times*, 24 Dec. 1000)

For a daily reminder of the pits into which careless interviewers may fall, the *Guardian's* corrections and clarifications column is unsurpassed.

Checking the relevance of what you're told is also important. Years ago a pram firm launched its own 'Pramway code, an aid for mothers: 10 ways to use a pram or pushchair safely'. After the press launch, all the nationals used it, printing the code in full. All except the *Guardian*. The *Guardian* reporter phoned the OPCS (now the ONS – Office for National Statistics) and asked how many accidents there had been involving prams in the last year. Answer: none. How many in last five years? Answer: none. So she wrote a totally different story, showing up the PR device for the sham it was.

You also need to be fair. As Matt Ridley wrote in the *Daily Telegraph*, 'The typical journalist's notion of balance is to quote an industrialist and Friends of the Earth, disenfranchising everybody in between.'

Sight of copy?

Showing interviewees copy before it's published is something many journalists say they won't do. They regard it as wimpish, an admission of inadequacy. But some journalists do – because it's part of the agreement, because they want to avoid trouble or because, with a complex, technical subject, they wish to ensure the facts are right.

Freelance Janet Barber remembers a profile she did for *She* magazine of the youngest local government chief executive in the country. 'He was 30 and completely stiff. He had a suit and spectacles and was completely respectable. I battled along with the interview but could not get the show on the road.' She did the best feature she could working from what she had.

The magazine sent the copy out for checking as it always did and the chief executive phoned her. He said: 'I realise this has got absolutely no personality about it. It's my fault. I'm new to this sort of thing. Would it be helpful if you could come back and talk to me again?' So she went back, had lunch with him, his wife and two of his children. This time she got a much more lively interview with more vivid details – like his usual breakfast, for instance: 'A Mars bar and a can of Coke'.

Editing quotes

Quotes are used to brighten copy, to emphasise a point, to move the story along, *not* because you want to fill space or show the world you can use a tape recorder.

How much do you change what interviewees say? As little as possible. Do you quote them accurately? Of course. Just as they know how to spell their own names, they know what words they use – so don't rewrite quotes without prior permission.

A journalist on a teen magazine asked a fashion PR for quotes on cut-price shopping. He remembers it clearly.

> 'She came round to interview me at home with a photographer who took pix around my flat. It was informal. We chatted and I told them all sorts of things which they obviously didn't write down in detail because when the interview came out I was horrified. [Quoting from the offending cutting:] "One looks so seedy . . ." I never use the word *one*. I despise it. They got the gist but didn't get the details right.
>
> Here, about shoes it says, "When they're scuffed or holey or worn down one looks so seedy and it's not so easy to get away with wearing second-hand clothes." I am sure I said something along those lines because it makes sense but it's not my language. What they printed is like girl talk. Here it says "I never use soap". Not true. "My skin's dry." It's not. "It's vital to moisturise my skin." I would have used more blokey talk.'

Contrary to received wisdom, most interviewees talk coherently. This is particularly true if the interviewer has focused their minds and asks precise questions. Disorganised people and very fast thinkers may give answers which jump about all over the place but in these days of media training they are fewer.

With most interviewees, then, the best guideline is tidy up, snip out 'ums' and 'ers' but never, ever change the sense. You can patch – take something they said at one point and link it with another sentence they used earlier – as long as you use their words and keep the meaning secure.

What if they said something vivid and quotable but not in a nice, neat, tidy sentence? There's no law that insists quotes must have subject, verb and object.

> '"As cuddly as a cut-throat razor," that was how Sir Peter Parker
> described . . .'

This has plenty of impact, probably more by being a snippet.

It's important to quote accurately, but do you quote *exactly* what people say? Let's start with swearing. If a pop star's every second word is 'fuck' or 'shit', do you print it? In a laddish mag, probably yes, though the frequency of swear words might be reduced, but you try to give a realistic impression of how the star talks. If the interview is for a family, middle-ground publication, then it's the editor's decision whether to use f*** and s**t. If the interview is for a sub-teen magazine, then probably not at all. It's possible to cut the swearing and yet keep quotes. The choice is to print accurately, cut or suggest. What is not acceptable is substituting a totally different word. You don't use 'excrement' in place of 'shit' or 'bonk' instead of 'fuck'.

What about correcting grammar? If an interviewee says 'Less than a thousand people turned up', would you change that to 'Fewer than a thousand people turned up'? I certainly wouldn't – unless the interviewee had said during the interview they'd like quotes tidied up or changed so they read grammatically. You're there to print what they said, not what the chief sub wished they'd said.

If the interviewee says, 'Not one of the nine reasons are valid,' do you change that to 'Not one of the nine reasons is valid?' Again, I'd say no. If you work on a writer's paper this should be acceptable. If you work on a sub's paper, it may well be changed. As the interviewer, you will know it's not what was said, your interviewee will know it's not what they said, but English grammar will have triumphed. As for changing quotes so they accord with house style – in the words of John McEnroe, 'You cannot be serious'.

However, since the prime reason for writing is to communicate, something has to be done if the interviewee uses obscure words.

> 'I can tell that's a clouded yellow butterfly by its jizz.'

Interesting but mystifying. You've got to explain what 'jizz' is and fairly quickly.

> 'I live in a duplex.'

Duplex? This is why square brackets were invented.

> 'I can tell a clouded yellow butterfly by its jizz [its flying pattern].'

> 'I live in a duplex [a maisonette].'

No changing quotes, please note, just clarifying them. 'You can presume intelligence but not knowledge' – one of the great journalistic principles.

If you reckon your interviewee knows what they are talking about, then – however weird the quote may be – either check it or leave it. Years ago,

I interviewed the famous American newspaperman Scott Newhall about a feud with a rival Californian editor who'd accused him in print of being a 'liberal' – an insupportable insult. Scott told me he had challenged the other editor to meet him under the Federal Savings and Loan clock at noon and defied him to 'repeat the slander'.

Back in Britain, I wavered and dithered. Obviously it was a libel not a slander. Should I change it or not? I couldn't reach Newhall and the deadline loomed, so eventually I decided he must have said it deliberately and used his words.

The story was picked up by *Press Gazette* and the writer made the point – which had completely missed me – that using the word 'slander' was an insult. The rival paper was so insignificant that no one read it, ergo the slur had to be slander.

Ridicule

Should you ridicule people by quoting exactly what they say? Only if you want to make a fool of them. If you interview someone you dislike heartily, a vainglorious prat who spends half the interview boasting about their love of classical music and then talks about 'Beethoven's Erotica Symphony', do you change that to 'Beethoven's Eroica Symphony'? Only you can decide. What you *don't* do is write 'Beethoven's Erotica Symphony [sic]'. You're the pompous prat then.

If they are incoherent and you don't wish to make a fool of them, your course is simple: turn what they say into reported speech. Don't succumb to the tyranny of the tape recorder.

Supposedly, the higher the position the person occupies, whether by election or selection, the more accustomed they become to criticism. Supposedly. It's a sad truth that very few of us can accurately judge what respect a person believes they deserve.

The capacity to be insulted is said to be directly and inversely related to intelligence. But the capacity to be offended by contested quotes in print is limitless. And if what you print is true, that just makes them more furious – with you.

'Sourcing'

When it comes to writing up a suspect statement or fact, 'source it' is the safest advice: i.e., attribute the statement to the speaker and put what's said inside quote marks. If you think it may be libellous, get a legal opinion.

'There's no truth in the rumour we're separating' is safer than 'They are not separating'. 'They said there was no truth in the rumour that they were separating' will do but lacks the immediacy of the quote. 'The marketing manager said, "Sales are 60 per cent up since March",' is wiser than reporting that 'the company's sales have risen 60 per cent over the last six months', though again 'The marketing manager reports that the company's sales have risen 60 per cent over the last six months' will do.

If you think people are lying to you, it's customary to source the quotes, writing 'claimed' instead of 'said' – a clear signal used by journalists that they don't believe the interviewee. But if you're writing about a business where nothing is straightforward and you're lied to for strategic purposes and almost every quote you include is doubtful, all those 'claims' would lose their potency. You need to accept that these are businesses where the readers are acutely aware of what's afoot, know how to interpret quotes, and revel in seeing what their opponents tell you.

Last word

Finally, what do you do when your interviewee 'doesn't trouble the note-taker'? Answer: You make the best of a bad job.

British reporter William Hall found Marlon Brando in his South Sea island hideaway. Marlon spoke perhaps five words to Hall before throwing him out. Did Hall despair? Of course not. He wrote a widely trumpeted feature about discovering Marlon Brando's South Sea island bolt hole. Lots of build up, lots of description, lots of 'there I woz . . .'

The entire interview consisted of less than one sentence – at that time one of the five words was unprintable.

7
Telephone interviewing

The telephone interview has been described as the McDonald's of journalism. 'Not the best method of gathering information but . . . fast and serviceable', according to American writer John Brady. Face-to-face interviewing is almost always preferable for all except routine calls but time and distance can dictate otherwise.

Interviewing on the telephone saves time and money – yours and theirs. Also, interviewees can't see you writing, so what they say is often less guarded. They can't see how far behind you are in note-taking or that you can't do shorthand so they worry less about what will appear in print.

But these advantages are nothing to what you lose. You can't see their reactions – a puzzled expression at a poorly phrased question, a twitch of annoyance at an ill-judged interruption or shuffling feet suggesting you are close to something sensitive. Neither can you see what they are doing: signing letters, opening their post or mouthing messages to colleagues across the office. You can't see the state of their desk, if they bite their nails, have a boringly corporate or rebellious tie, designer stubble or a mad professor haircut.

If it's impersonal for you, it's also impersonal for them. Without the benefit of smiles or flattering eye contact you have to work harder to lock on to their interest and retain their attention. Because you can't see the signs of boredom, you may plod on with a line of questioning that's dangerously unproductive. Because you can't see puzzlement, you might fail to clarify answers and so misunderstand or misinterpret what's said.

You also have to guard against extraneous 'noises off' coming from where you work distracting or mystifying your interviewee. Newspaper and magazine offices are not quite the Animal Houses of years gone by, but if you have boisterous colleagues it's a good idea to conduct phone interviews at the quietest time or in a special room set aside for the purpose. It is, or should be, a rule in offices never to talk to a fellow journalist during a telephone interview.

Mouthing important messages, yes. Scribbling comments, yes. But shouting so the interviewee on the other end can hear, certainly not.

What you have to work with is your voice, your charm, your persuasiveness – that ability to convince your interviewee that it's in their interest to talk to you. This is where you're greatly helped, if you're fortunate, by the prestige of your publication; where being staff/freelance for the *Daily Mail*, *Financial Times* or *New Scientist* scores. If by contrast you work for an unknown or zero-rated publication, you'll have ample opportunity to practise persuasion. You also need an ear to judge your interviewee's reactions, working solely from the sound of their voice: its pitch, volume, speed, accent; from the hesitations, pauses, silences, words used and words avoided.

Some people have an easy telephone manner. They're unfazed by having to talk to someone they don't know, have never met, didn't even know existed. The best guide to how you play on the telephone is social and sexual. If you've ever been chatted up and asked out by someone you've never met, or done the chatting up and been accepted, then the odds are you communicate easily and well.

For print journalists, perception, intelligence and approach matter more than voices. A plummy or gorblimey accent can be a hindrance – but noticeably isn't when allied with talent. Probably the most important thing is to like talking on the phone. The more sophisticated may cringe at what follows but it really is worth saying: *smile when you dial*.

Telephone manners

First impressions count on the telephone just as much as they do face to face. The best advice is to introduce yourself straightaway. If you're a trade journalist phoning anywhere outside the UK in the English-speaking world, it's wise first to say your name and that you're a reporter or writer before you mention your publication.

If you start the other way round, you may well be mistaken for a space seller and given the bum's rush. Having to talk your way through that initial barrier makes you admire the space seller's persistence and ability to get through in the face of hostility.

If you're telephoning and hoping to get through and talk in English to non-English speakers, advice varies depending on your linguistic ability. If you're not at home in their language, the best bet when the operator answers is to say slowly and clearly and repeat if necessary: 'Do you speak English, please?' When you get through to someone who does, then it's probably best to start with your publication's name, since that should be more easily recognised.

Once that's established, make it clear you're a writer and who you wish to talk to. If you're fluent in the language of your interviewee, there should be no problem.

When you get through to the person you wish to talk to (establishing that and reaching them is covered later), then it's important to check that it's a convenient time to talk. Try something along the following lines: 'I'd be grateful for a couple of minutes of your time' or 'Could you spare me a few minutes?' If you don't, you really could set off on the wrong foot. Your interviewee may be in the middle of a meeting and the more you push on with the interview, the more impatience and annoyance build up at their end. If your potential interviewee makes it clear they can spare just a few minutes, then pitch in with some good questions, outline what areas you'd like to explore and fix a suitable time to talk again. 'I'd like to go through this in much greater detail. Is there a convenient time to phone back?'

Ignore this advice only if you have been chasing a truly elusive interviewee who seems to have been deliberately avoiding you but suddenly answers the phone. Then pile in straightaway and don't offer them an escape route *of any sort*. Remember that very few people ever put the phone down on an interviewer; it's never happened to me or any of the reporters and feature writers I know. This is where you push your luck. If you give the elusive a chance to defer an interview they don't want to do, they'll grab it.

Preparation

This needs to be even more thorough than for face-to-face interviews for all the reasons cited earlier. You should complete your research and know what you want to get out of the interview before you pick up the phone. Because telephone interviews tend to be shorter than face-to-facers, one way to save yourself time is to frame some questions to make it clear that you are conversant with certain areas of the subject so that they don't have to go over them again.

All the necessary topics to be covered should be written down in a logical asking sequence and, as before, on a separate piece of paper. Make sure the must-knows are included. The questions need to be simple, clear and unambiguous. If you have any doubts about the answers, check. 'So what you're saying is . . .?'

It's important not to rush telephone interviews at the end, even if your interviewee appears to be in a hurry to ring off. Quickly review your questions to check you've asked everything and glance back over your notes, to check you've clarified any queries. Going back again later to check is embarrassing and somehow destroys any established relationship. Because telephone interviews are shorter, they seem to be on a more superficial level – usually to establish facts and opinions – so to have to go back implies poor organisation and sloppy reporting.

Getting through

Research should show who to talk to and where they are. If it's in the UK, reaching the interviewee's office/workplace should be simple, particularly if you have discovered their direct line. If not, ring the firm, factory or office and ask to be put through to them, by name and title: 'Charles Morris, managing director, please.' This is useful should Morris have quit or been booted out a few days previously.

Unless you feel your interviewee may be reluctant to talk to you, if asked you should give the operator your name. You'll probably be asked who you are again by the secretary or PA. Just be patient, polite and firm and don't let any exasperation show. Would you talk to every journo who rang?

Explain again where you're from and that the interview is important and/or urgent, but at this point the best advice is not to say what you want to talk about in detail. If you do, you're into negotiation through a third party which can drag out far too long for comfort. Have a proper sense of your publication and its importance.

If you come across a dragon secretary/PA puffed with self-importance guarding access to your chosen interviewee, it's tempting to get heavy or dismissive. Don't. Continue to ask to be put through or to discover when the interviewee will be free. If asked to phone back at a certain time, do so. Continue once, twice, thrice – but if it goes on too long or too close to deadline the most effective ploy is to ask directly: 'Look – am I being put off? Will they ever talk to me? I need to know.' This usually gets an answer and in my experience it's 'Yes, they will talk to you. Just a moment.'

Remember that secretaries/PAs who guard so zealously are usually reflecting the demands of an insecure boss who wants to be protected. This insecurity also means they don't want to be seen as insecure, so faced with 'Are they avoiding me?' the secretary will generally opt for 'Of course not', followed by more questions about what you want to ask. This is a signal to be reassuringly bland.

Another approach is to realise that secretaries/PAs often arrive later and leave earlier than their bosses, so if you phone before 8.30am or after 5.30pm you may get through to the boss direct.

Another ploy is to ask for their deputy and here you can explain what you're after. Directly or indirectly you'll probably get a good idea of the chances of getting an interview this way.

Answerphone or voice mail on all the time? Infuriating, but persevere with a two-pronged approach. One method is to leave several messages along the lines of 'Hope to talk to you before Thursday noon, which is my deadline', being sure to phone at least three times on Thursday morning. Then phone back Thursday afternoon when they think it's all over and have stopped playing invisible to say 'So relieved to catch you. I have an extended deadline.'

The other, less kind approach is to phone their boss with great concern that the interviewee appears to be absent and you are concerned about their health.

Techniques

In telephone interviews, grunts, 'uh-huhs' and 'yeses' take the place of nods and smiles. You have to let your interviewee know you are listening. If you doubt this, the next time a good friend phones, just listen. After a minute or two they'll hesitate, stop, then say: 'Are you there?' You have to encourage your interviewee to keep on talking. This is the key – they talk, you listen. If there are silences, don't fill them (except with an encouraging 'uh-uh').

The techniques are really the same as for face-to-face interviews but without the subtler ploys that require a reading of the physical response. You should try to establish a businesslike and/or friendly working relationship. If you can establish common ground, so much the better. Start by giving them a very clear idea of what you want to talk about, so they can collect their thoughts.

Questions should be simple, so they can't be misunderstood. Never interrupt or, if by ill chance you do, stop at once.

When you're interviewing on the telephone, it doesn't matter if you're wearing dirty jeans, or smoking, or if your fingernails are black from gardening. What does matter is whether you sit, particularly if it's a tricky call. If you think you're likely to have trouble getting through, stand up. You'll be more dominant. This old space-seller's trick works. If you don't believe it, try it.

The best type of telephone is a hands-free headset with earpiece and mouthpiece. This saves 'reporter's crook-neck' and 'reporter's weary ear'. If you're freelance, opt for one that has a dialling print-out, call timer and call waiting display.

Recording

Recording telephone interviews makes good sense. Because interviewees can't see you scribbling away, they tend to talk fast; slowing them down is difficult and stops the flow. These interviews also tend to be shorter than face-to-facers so there's less to listen back to or transcribe. Recording interviews means you don't need to take notes; this gets round the embarrassing situation of having to go back afterwards if there's something in your notes you can't read.

There are several ways to tape: attach a mike-lead from a tape recorder to your headset, plug a special tape recorder into the phone socket or use the recording facility on an answerphone. Either way, practise first. If you worry about the recording acoustic being audible, let your interviewee know you are recording them.

The law in Britain is that if one party knows the recording is being made, that's OK. Trouble starts if neither knows a recording is being made, i.e., it's being made covertly.

Interviewing abroad

I spent three years as a business correspondent for an international duty-free magazine and every month conducted telephone interviews world-wide, all, I feel ashamed to say, in English. My least favourite places to write about were Singapore and Hong Kong, since peak interview time was midnight to 2.30am.

It taught me a lot. First, to use a form of basic English. No slang, no metaphors, no jazzy idioms, no new words. It taught me to repeat back what I was told, to check I'd understood correctly. It taught me a lot about geography and how wonderful *Economist* guides are.

Most of all it taught me to say *something* in my interviewee's language. I can say 'Thank you' in Finnish (*kiitos*) and Japanese (*arigato*) and you'd be surprised how useful they have been. They helped establish rapport. I was a stereotypical monoglot Brit but I made an effort. My efforts made my interviewee laugh: as everyone knows, do that and you're halfway there.

8
Note-taking and recording

Journalists make notes so they can write accurate stories containing the required mix of facts, colour, background, anecdotes and quotes. They aim to avoid those dread words: 'There's been a complaint . . .'

To make notes they use shorthand, longhand scribble, tape recorder or memory. Which they opt for is a trade-off between what they want from the interview, the skills they possess, the time available and the sensitivity or temperament of the interviewee. For interviewees they know well, journalists can walk in carrying an open notebook. With the elusive or reclusive, they may decide not to bring out a tape recorder until they judge their interviewee has relaxed.

Some write reams during the interview, some write nothing. Some write surreptitiously on notebooks under the table or even in their jacket pockets, though how readable jacket-pocket notes are is debatable. There are investigative reporters who are 'wired' for sound and vision.

Each approach has its strengths and drawbacks, but there are two enduring principles. First, few journalists regret learning shorthand. What they regret is letting it rust. Second, however good you think your memory is, it's fallible, so don't overstretch it.

Unfortunately, there's no one best method. It all depends what you're after. If it's a 2,000-word profile of a rising celebrity, requiring good quotes and plenty of description to be delivered in two weeks, then tape recorder and notebook used in tandem will probably work best. If what's wanted is a 200-word news story, deadline in an hour, then use shorthand. For an anecdote from a nervous friend of an about-to-be-convicted criminal? Memory, with story committed to notebook asap.

Electronic

Tape recorders are popular with journalists because of the protection they afford, less so with certain interviewees. They are great for face-to-face profiles. Mini 'snoop/spy' video cameras, which film from inside sports bags, now form part of many investigative reporters' equipment.

Tape recorders

For:

- Provide proof of what was said. 'To err is human, to get it on tape divine' is said to be the motto of *News of the World* investigative reporters.
- You get the feeling of truth into your quotes.
- Enable you to concentrate on your interviewee and establish excellent eye contact.
- Most interviewees soon forget they're being taped and talk freely.
- If the interviewee is a fast talker, you don't have to slow them down to get the quotes.
- Editors trust them.
- Interviewees who know they have been taped rarely question the accuracy of quotes.
- You can interview in a car or other moving object where writing may be difficult.

Against:

- You can't record gestures, the colour of the interviewee's eyes, state of the desk or ambience.
- Not suitable for group interviews.
- Batteries can go flat.
- Tape can run out.
- Some don't work particularly well in noisy places such as restaurants or factories.
- Tapes take hours to transcribe.
- You may have to listen many times.
- Seem to encourage over-quoting, often of banal words.
- Bulky to store.

Some negative aspects can easily be countered: ensuring the batteries are new, for instance, and checking the tape occasionally. If you have a recorder with a counter and cue marker, it shouldn't be necessary to listen back several times. Just listen once and mark the best quotes, then you can go straight to them later.

The reluctant interviewee is more difficult. In business journalism it's usually only villains who object to being recorded but elsewhere there are some inexperienced, nervous, often older, interviewees who genuinely experience mike fright. Time for persuasion and sweet-talk.

Always go for a recorder with an indicator light to show it's working and a counter. If most of your interviews are single-person face-to-face, ensure the recorder has a unidirectional mike. An omni-directional mike will probably pick up far too much extraneous sound, particularly in restaurants or crowded rooms.

If you have a voice-activated recording facility on your recorder, ensure it's permanently taped off and if you carry your tape recorder in a packed bag, make certain the play/record facility is locked off, too, or you could arrive with flat batteries.

The hand-held standard-size cassette recorder has the advantage over the mini-cassette recorder that tapes are cheap, obtainable all over the country and can be played back off the mains without flatting the batteries.

Written

Interviewees do not want to be misquoted, so are reassured to see a notebook. There's no need to apologise when you produce one: it's the journalist's calling card. But produce it at the right time, use it properly and don't lose it. Pens or ballpoints with permanent ink are advisable.

Daft as it may sound to beginners, there really is one best way of using a spiral bound 'reporter's' notebook and that is to go right the way through on one side of the paper to the end and, providing it's good quality paper, then turn the book over and come back. Once you've started writing, turning the *book* rather than the paper is a recipe for disaster.

Every interview must be dated and it's not a bad idea to make a contents list on the inside front and inside back covers. This helps to locate interviews should you need to refer to them again. Don't rip pages out of your notebook. It's a bad habit to get into and could destroy proof of what an interviewee had said and give the appearance of tampering with evidence.

What size notebook? For face-to-face, anything except A4 which is too big, too floppy, intimidating and hard to use. Bound or spiral-bound A5 notebooks suit many reporters but seem to be losing ground to smaller A6 books, which can be put in a jacket pocket or handbag so the briefcase or monstrous bag can be left at home.

For telephone interviews, when you don't need to keep your notes shielded, an A4 pad on your desk works well. If you are recording a telephone interview, then use the memo facility of a tape, not digital, answerphone or a special attachment on the earpiece of the handset attached to your tape recorder.

Advice for beginners: don't put the questions down in your notebook leaving space underneath for the answers. Answers are never the length estimated and doing this ties you into a sequence, inhibiting those all important follow-up questions. Always have your questions separate. It's not a bad idea to devise some sort of code you can use for an instant edit while you make notes. Two lines by the side of a good quote, for instance; a cross to show you need to go back again for more information.

Because so much is going on during an interview – listening to answers, checking for consistency, appraising, planning future questions and making notes as well – it's worth considering keeping a running note of what has to be checked when an opportunity arises, without interrupting or spoiling the flow.

As they occur to you, write the key points to be checked at the top of the page. As you turn over, if you haven't managed to have them answered, carry them over until the opportunity arises. The alternative is to mark in the margin areas you think you'll need to return to later and towards the end of the interview scan your notes to check what remains to be clarified.

Longhand scribble

For:

- Simple.
- OK with a very, very slow speaker, perhaps; or where you're interviewing in a foreign language and everything is translated from English into another language and then back again.
- Just about suitable for statistics, short facts.

Against:

- Slow.
- Unimpressive.
- Relies heavily on memory.
- Not good for lively quotes.
- Advice: only if you must – much better to learn Teeline.

Shorthand

For:

- Minimal, inexpensive equipment.
- Works almost everywhere, unhampered by noise, magnets, being dropped, etc.
- Immediately accessible, i.e., no need to rewind and listen back.
- Acceptable in law.
- Some interviewees impressed, ditto colleagues, looks good on CVs.
- About four to five times faster than longhand.

Against:

- Takes time to learn.
- Minimises eye contact.
- Looks old-fashioned to some interviewees, particularly celebrities.
- Unless notetaker is very skilled, needs to be read back quickly.
- Unlike tapes, not verbatim.
- Chance of errors both in note-taking and transcription.

The main shorthand systems taught in the English-speaking world are, in order of invention, Gregg, Pitman's New Era, Speedwriting, Teeline and Pitman 2000. Generally speaking, the easier a system is to learn, the longer it will take to write. What makes a system easy to learn is simple theory and a light memory load (not too many short forms). What holds you up is complicated theory, when you have to stop and think: 'Is that written up or down, with a loop or a hook?'

However, it's reading it back that counts and here if the theory is simple and the vowels are included in what's written down, it's generally easy to read back. The more the system depends on placement on or above the line, on thick or thin strokes and on short forms, then the harder it is to read back.

The system favoured by most British journalists is Teeline, invented in 1967 by journalist James Hill who was unhappy with existing choices. The memory load is light and the theory can be learnt in 20 hours. Shorthand teacher Patricia Hampton says her Teeline students reach 100wpm within a term, doing shorthand just six or seven hours a week for 12 weeks. Some trainees on the PMA postgraduate nine-week journalism course taught by her reach 100wpm in just under 30 hours. Top achievable speeds with Teeline are 130–140wpm, quite enough for most working journos.

This is a system vaunted for its accuracy and taught by the BBC and on NCTJ courses. Students attaining 100 per cent accuracy with Teeline are said to outnumber other systems' students by four to one. Its critics say it's too flexible, allowing people to develop their own version. Others think this a plus. The recommended book is *Teeline Fast* by Ann Dix. 'Nothing comes anywhere near it,' says Hampton.

Pitman 2000 has a ceiling speed of 120–130wpm and a middling heavy memory load (83 short forms). However, it has all the problems of a system based on the fountain pen, where thick and thin strokes and placement on above or below the line are critical. If you're using a ballpoint pen on unlined paper, one shape could be read as 'see' or 'easy' 'ass' or 'essay', and because Pitman's is a phonetic rather than alphabetic system, it can be a handicap when interviewing in a foreign language – as I discovered when I interviewed a Japanese cognac blender in French. There was the added complication of the Japanese inability to pronounce the letter L. Experiences like these teach you to take a tape recorder as well.

For journalists who need shorthand of 130wpm and above, there are two choices: Pitman New Era with ceiling speeds of 250wpm and Gregg Simplified, ceiling speed 200wpm. Pitman New Era, launched in 1922, has fairly complex theory, a very heavy memory load of 400 short forms and relies on placement, thick and thin strokes and omitting vowels at speed.

Parliamentary reporters working for *Hansard* take notes for about 10 minutes at a stretch, some using Pitman's New Era, others stenographic machines, yet others transcribing from tapes. Of those who use shorthand, around 80 per cent have such a precise 'note' it can be read back by others.

Sadly, Gregg Simplified, though widespread in the US, has to be ruled out in Britain except by the determined who can track down the few enthusiastic and dedicated Gregg teachers, who like its integral vowels and the fact that once a rule is learnt it is never modified. It would have taken hold in Britain but for the Americans. Dr John Gregg, the Irishman who developed it, went off to the US in 1893 when he discovered someone was going to bring out his system in Chicago under another name. He never returned.

Speedwriting has an 80–100wpm ceiling. It's easy to learn but takes huge effort to get up to any speed so is not suitable for most journalists.

You should use shorthand for facts, comments and really good quotes – not for every word. That just causes extra work reading back, weary wrists and overfull notebooks. An expense of spirit in wasteful action.

It takes time and practice with shorthand not to take down too much. You have to learn to edit as you go along. This comes from knowing your brief, and understanding what interests the readers. Reports and features crammed with too many quotes are often indigestible.

Whether you're left-handed or right-handed makes no difference to the ability to write shorthand. What does make a difference is IQ and mind-set. Shorthand expert Harry Butler has said that the analytical can have problems.

If you want to know your shorthand potential, here's a do-it-yourself aptitude test. Type a few paragraphs (at least 50 words) and print out in at least double spacing. Then ask a friend to time you or time yourself and see how many words you can write in the space of a minute under the printed words.

> If you've written 40–50 words, your speed potential is 120wpm.
>
> If you've written about 35 words, your potential is 100wpm.
>
> If you've written about 25 words, your potential is 80wpm.

A final thought about shorthand. At an aviation press conference a journalist from *Travel Trade Gazette* found that her pen had run out.

> 'I went through my bag and realised I hadn't a spare. I'd left the office in a hurry and there was nobody there I knew to borrow from. I rooted around and found my eyeliner. I used it as the lightest possible shorthand.'

And yes, 'they used the story'. You couldn't have done that with longhand.

Slow, slow, quick, quick, slow

There are bound to be times when your notetaking lags. How you buy time is your choice. Some journalists advise throwing in a soft 'filler' question and just not listening to the answer while you write on. Easier said than done. Others repeat back with admiration or amazement the answer or quote they are busy writing down. Yet again, others say: 'Sorry, you're going a little fast. Would you hold on a second please?'

Reading back

The rule is to read back your notes as soon as possible, certainly within a few hours, while your memory of the interview is still fresh. You'll be glad you did. Short-term memory fades quickly and another, intervening interview can drive recollection of strange words or speech patterns clean out of your head. So don't let the sun go down on your unread notebook.

Memory

For:

- Puts nervous interviewees at ease (but worries experienced interviewees who will wonder how good your memory is).
- Relaxed, chatty interviewees often give better quotes.

Against:

- Memory is notoriously and demonstrably unreliable.
- Unless notes are made immediately afterwards, they are vulnerable to attack in a court of law.

Actors and counsellors, who have been trained to remember, do well at recalling conversations; most journalists less so. Reporters' confidence in their memory over a protracted interview is usually misplaced. That doesn't mean you should always have your notebook in your hand. When you first meet someone, before the interview proper has begun, your interviewee may say something eminently quotable. Remember it and write it down as soon as you get your notebook out.

Again, at the end of the interview, when you've put your notebook away and are just chatting, your interviewee may let slip some valuable information. Don't hoick your notebook out, but take the first opportunity after leaving to write it down. Note the time, too.

Notes made immediately afterwards are acceptable in court. Memory is much more likely to be probed and put to the test. Police notes are accepted as evidence so there's no reason for journalists to be defensive about relying on shorthand.

9
Different interviewees
Politicians

As interviewees, politicians are a breed apart. Even experienced journalists rate them as difficult and for good reason: most politicians are wary, guileful and well trained. My first interview with an MP ended with him slowly and distinctly dictating his thoughts to me, watching as I took down every word in shorthand. I still cringe at the memory.

If you want to succeed at interviewing politicians, you have to go back and analyse the whole process, from the historical evolution of political interviews to how today's politicians see and use the media. First, remind yourself what the political interview is meant to represent. Even with today's technology, there's no way a politician, minister or local councillor can talk to all the voters. Historically, the journalist's role was to ask the searching questions that intelligent voters would ask if they had the chance. Unfortunately, that long ago became distorted, as today's political journalists will testify.

With spin-doctors and sophisticated news management, it's now harder to question politicians effectively. However, it remains essential, because politics is one of the most important aspects of life and needs to be taken seriously. It's also one area where journalists can contribute to the democratic process.

Empathise

Harold Frayman of the *Observer* has worked with politicians for more than 20 years. He says: 'The biggest problem for journalists trying to interview politicians, whether local councillors or ministers, is that most journalists can't put themselves in politicians' shoes. They can't empathise.' If they did they might realise how difficult being a politician is.

He compares politics with business, where you may be subject to a vicious campaign attacking what you're doing. Your customers may drift away but over time you have a chance to put things right. Should people boycott your product, you can develop others. 'But politicians' customers vote on one occasion, all at one time,' Frayman says. 'All your opponent needs is a simple majority and then you haven't just lost that product, you've lost the world.'

Probably more than any other group, politicians feel under attack. They have reason, being one of the least trusted groups in society; they're not considered to be caring or sincere. Yet carrying this burden of public distrust and disapproval, they're obliged by law to publish details of decisions and transcripts of debates. As Frayman explains:

> 'They have to do things in public, but they don't like it any more than anyone else would. . . . The truth is that most politicians, however cynical, however ambitious, are motivated by a public interest more than a selfish interest. I'm not saying there's no self-interest, but they do want to do something positive. They do want to change the world for the better.'

Lies, damn lies

And what do politicians find when interviewed by journalists? Far too often they're quizzed either by unbriefed, poorly trained pushovers who waste their precious time, or by crusading reporters and feature writers determined to nail them with the old, old question resonating in their heads: 'Why is this lying bastard lying to me?' As Frayman says:

> 'Of course politicians lie, but no more than most people. There's nothing about being a politician that makes them naturally more inclined to be dishonest, but they end up stating as a fact what they actually hope will happen.'

Or to put it another way, politicians have a tendency to speak only partial truth, for 'politics would often be impossible without public reticence' – diplomatic language from former *Guardian* deputy editor John Cole.

When dealing with the press, politicians are aware, above all, of the vital importance of perception. They work energetically to project a positive image and never forget that unless cleverly handled, careless comments may pitch them into a black hole. One serious gaffe can hold back advancement or, at worst, destroy a career – less easily now, perhaps, but it happens. More than almost any group they know the value of publicity and the power of the media.

Wilson's punch

First, a look at how politicians have been treated in this country in the lifetime of present MPs – a deliberately chosen timeframe. Though politicians couldn't survive if they didn't adapt to changing circumstances, there's no doubt they instinctively react well to approaches they feel comfortable with.

'Is there anything else you'd like to tell the nation, prime minister?' was the deferential approach 70 years ago. After the Second World War, though still treating politicians with respect, journalists began to ask more pertinent questions and receive more carefully thought-out answers. Deference slowly receded, though as late as 1970 Harold Wilson punched the young John Simpson, who dared to approach him to ask about a possible general election date.

The event is dramatically recorded in Simpson's book *Strange Places, Questionable People* (1998). It was on his first day in his new job as a reporter. Wilson was off to his Liverpool constituency, where it was thought he might announce a general election. Downing Street had offered a photo call at Euston Station. Simpson didn't realise there was an unwritten rule about when reporters did – and did not – question prime ministers. He writes:

> The reporters waiting for him [Wilson] on Platform 7 smiled ingratiat-
> ingly, as they tend to do when the great ones of the earth pass their way.
> I glanced around and realised smiling was all they meant to do. . . .
> [Simpson stepped forward.] "Excuse me, prime minister . . ." My entire
> world exploded.

He doubled up with pain from the punch. The event was witnessed by many other journalists and was photographed but never reported.

The sharper questions of the 1960s resulted in fuller answers, and fuller answers led to more probing and forceful questions. Maybe it was the reporting on Watergate in the United States, forcing President Nixon's resignation, coupled with the arrival of the *Sun* in Britain that heralded the beginning of the end of press deference. On TV, interviews became adversarial; in print they became tougher and rougher.

Politicians began to employ consultants who advised on everything from hair-styles to hand movements, from when to lie low to when to schmooze, from when to attack to when to make pre-emptive confessions.

Study your quarry

By a process of natural selection, today's politicians are fit and equipped with the attributes and techniques necessary to defend themselves against the assaults of the press. So a study of your quarry is essential and the word 'quarry' is deliberately chosen. Few other interviewees today are so skilful or need such a careful, well-planned approach.

It's important to understand the way they think, which is not how journal-ists think. Journalists' priority is to pass on facts and comment. Politicians' priority is to achieve the result they seek.

Just as it's hard for journalists to understand politicians, it's often difficult, says Frayman, for politicians to understand journalists.

> 'They don't seem to be able to learn that if you don't want people to know something, the best way is not to tell them. They think they can win favours by passing on little titbits just for you and are astonished when they start turning up in print.'

The question they ask themselves

Politicians may divide into right-wing or left-wing, tough or tender, ideologues or pragmatists, but the question they all ask themselves when being interviewed is: 'How will my words play in print?'

Their most precious asset is how much they know. Information is power and they are on the inside. Robin Corbett, now MP for Birmingham Erdington and previously a journalist, put it succinctly when asked why he's not worried about being caught out by journalists: 'I know far more about the subject than they do.'

Politics is their life and their business and it's one that's conducted for much of the time person-to-person, face-to-face in areas of Parliament or the local council chambers where journalists can't roam at will. Also, politicians are by nature adept manoeuvrers, adroit at side-stepping, ducking and weaving – skills they refine after endless practice at selection committees, party events, debates, meetings, meetings, meetings, interviews, interviews, interviews.

Because they're supremely outcome-oriented, they analyse the results of these meetings and interviews, learning all the time, tweaking and perfecting their responses. They learn to be close observers, acute judges of human nature and quick on the uptake.

Practice sessions

Training, formal or informal, is freely available to politicians and 'prepping' is a way of life. Experienced journalists often take part in these training sessions, giving politicians practice at what to expect. Harold Frayman, then with *Labour Weekly*, remembers a Labour Party press conference training exercise with a female politician who later became a junior minister.

> 'We asked her the sort of questions she'd be asked at the by-election. The point was to show her how it could be, to prepare her for the ordeal ahead, and I suspect it did. But she never talked to me again politely. She'd been made to look a fool inside a private room and she couldn't stand it. I didn't regard it as a failure on her part but she couldn't forgive the pain. There was no need for blame, just a need for her to learn.'

Buffers and bruisers

With the emergence of spin-doctors, politicians have become even harder to reach and outsmart. 'It's useful for politicians to have someone who will stand between them and the journalists and do the shouting, which they perceive to be necessary,' Frayman says, 'because bullying works.'

With an experienced politician, all these defences are in place before a single journalistic question is asked. It's then they activate their formidable interview techniques, which for some include 30 different ways of not answering the question without refusing to do so point blank (see p. 106).

But first, who's up against them in this apparently unequal contest? At national daily paper level, the contest is not quite so unequal. Specialists such as lobby correspondents, gallery reporters, political editors and reporters covering areas such as labour relations, health and education are journalists with years of experience, who talk to politicians of every party at every level. Politicians, combative by nature, enjoy sparring with these experts, to whom politics is exciting and supremely important.

National reporters have the advantage that they can parcel out contact with politicians to suit themselves. If a particular reporter gets on well with one minister, that's fine. And if that minister tells their contact a story they shouldn't, well, the contact can pass it on so that it appears under a different byline. 'Then,' says Frayman, 'the reporter if questioned can say to the minister "I don't know where they got that story from. It wasn't me!"'

Style and substance

You're not on radio or TV, so don't model your style on John Humphrys or Jeremy Paxman. The dynamics of interviewing for print are completely different. TV thrives on agreed and staged conflict. Remember that the politicians have agreed to appear and have most likely cleared the subjects they will be questioned on. Radio thrives on quick-fire exchange.

For print you should adopt a more subtle approach. The interviewers politicians dislike are the poorly prepared, the lazy, the untrained. The late Sir Robin Day, who'd spent a lifetime obsessed with interviews, put it neatly in his memoirs: 'Politicians like vigorous, well-informed questions. Training and experience make them responsive to such questioning. A limp, flabby and ill-informed interview does not stimulate them.'

Robin Corbett says: 'The worst are the bone idle, the ones who haven't done their homework, who walk in and ask: "Are you a member of any committee, Mr Corbett?"' (He's Chairman of the powerful Home Affairs Select Committee.) 'Or they don't know about local transport campaigns that we've been running for years. I go mad about it.' He says that some of the worst offenders are on weekly papers and he questions their induction process. He doesn't expect trainee reporters to be local experts immediately, but says it's important they find out what's going on in the district: who's the largest local employer, what local concerns are and so on.

'They don't get out of the office enough. They don't know the local councillors or where they drink. Papers are run like fire stations: reporters leave only when the alarm bells ring. I find it stupid.' There are stories everywhere, right on their doorstep, he says, if only reporters would look.

Techniques for journalists

Politicians are astute, informed and motivated and will gladly tell you at length what they want you to know. The skill is luring them to tell what they'd rather you *didn't* know, either now, later or for ever. The journalist usually knows what the politician's message is likely to be and will probably be bored, having heard it before. The politician suspects, often correctly, that the journalist doesn't want to hear it.

What can the journalist do when faced with embattled individuals, equipped with well-practised defence strategies? The repertoire of possible approaches ranges from make friends/become trusted at one extreme to dish the dirt/go nuclear at the other.

As ever, go in well-researched and with empathy. Politicians may, of course, at the outset try to throw you, make you feel uncomfortable, but that's unlikely at a first meeting. Then they are likely to take your measure. The advice from a government press officer who for several years sat in on ministerial interviews is: 'Know your stuff. Politicians, whatever party, don't want to be interviewed by fools who haven't done their homework. They can tell from the first few questions what the journalist's agenda is and how clued up they are.' His advice is to let politicians ramble on a little at first and listen to what they say for two reasons: first to accord them recognition of their power, second in order to ask supplementary questions. Certainly, he advises, never present your own politics.

The really adroit political journalist, he says, knows who each politician is friendly with and who they sit next to in the House of Commons or House of Lords. 'I like politicians because it's such a clever profession, so skilful,' he says. 'They know they're powerful and that it doesn't go on for ever. It's all about presentation, acting, putting on a show.' Far too many young journalists, he says, put on dismal performances. 'I'm astounded by the stupidity of some young reporters: so ill-informed I wonder how they are ever going to write a story about anything.'

Softly, softly

'Putting politicians at their ease is not simple,' Frayman says, 'because if they're any good at being a politician they're not going to relax.' Start with simple questions that they find easy to answer. Politicians are no exception to that rule, though asking how they spell their names is not a good idea. Checking might be permissible with parish councillors or candidates from obscure parties, not otherwise.

Trainee local paper reporters should set out to establish a good relationship with their local MPs right away. Remember that almost every politician you talk to will be an experienced interviewee and won't be impressed if you arrive late, haven't brought a pen or forget to bring spare batteries for your tape recorder.

Your immediate imperative is to get the story and your first objective should be to convince them of your ability to report accurately. 'You'll get more if you sound as though you are basically in tune with what they are saying,' says Frayman. 'Being combative just reminds them the chances are the interview could do them damage.'

That doesn't mean you gush enthusiastically when being told of their plans for improving litter bins, but it does mean you show you are listening and understand what they're saying and ask intelligent questions be they Conservative, Labour, Liberal Democrat, Natural Law or Monster Raving Loony Party.

A sympathetic, understanding response often produces a better result than direct questioning. Saying, 'Yes, and I suppose . . .' shows you understand what they are driving at, Frayman says. It reassures them too, which is very important during early interviews, because being misunderstood and misquoted is a standard fear.

If your reports are accurate, they will remember and should be happy to talk to you again. After one or two more meetings they may offer you something fairly tempting 'off the record'. If you want them to trust you – and it's very much in your interest that they do – it's important to establish that you both understand exactly what that means: information 'off the record' is something you agree not to print.

If they won't change to 'unattributable' – information you can print but without identifying the source – then either switch off the tape recorder, put down your pen or make a very, very clear mark in your notebook indicating what is 'off the record'. When you type back your notes, put that info on a separate page, store it separately and *don't* print it.

Gaining trust is like a ritual mating dance. It takes time, is neither easily established nor lightly given. Protestations by the journalist such as 'You can trust me – I won't tell a soul' are counter-productive, since they give the opposite impression. Report accurately, don't betray confidences, and trust should begin to develop.

Follow up

Robin Corbett's advice for all non-specialist reporters who deal with politicians, besides do your homework, is: follow up what you're told. 'I can count on the fingers of one hand the number of times in 25 years in Parliament that reporters have actually followed up comments such as "I'm so upset about this I'm going to write to the prime minister."' All it takes is a phone call and one question: 'What happened?'

Local paper reporters are particularly well placed to be fed with excellent stories if they show they understand politicians and their priorities. But why should MPs bother with an untrained reporter, whose previous interview was a waste of time, when a well-written press release would (a) be more accurate; (b) probably be printed almost in its entirety; and (c) would save them time and trouble? The obvious answer is that they need to be elected and keep in with the press, who can help or harm them – but they also know that the press can be vindictive if slighted or scorned. So requests for interviews will be turned down with sadness and the hope there'll be time in the future – which will arrive nearer election times.

Distractions

Being pushed too much by journalists makes politicians jumpy. Feeling under attack triggers exactly the reaction the journalist doesn't want: up go the defences. For any chance to succeed you need to be aware of the techniques they may use against you.

If your questions approach an area they don't want to discuss, distractions include:

- red herring (a diverting – in both senses – snippet dangled enticingly before the journalist's nose)
- put-down (a barely disguised insult designed to wrong-foot the journalist and make them defensive)
- word-bridging and looping (smoothly slipping away from a subject they don't want to discuss on to one they do)
- steamroller (carry on regardless of question, interjection, raised pen, raised eyebrows, any attempt by interviewer to speak)
- 'please stop accusing me' (a favourite of Mrs T's)

- 'I'm glad you asked me that' (long-winded explanation that goes absolutely nowhere)
- treats and titbits (rewards for good behaviour – they come with a price-tag attached
- flat refusal (much the hardest to combat).

'But answer came there none . . .'

Politicians avoid answering difficult questions in countless ways but their ploys break down into nine main categories, with at least three times that number of variants. The main categories are to:

- ignore the question
- acknowledge the question without answering
- question the question
- attack the question
- decline to answer
- make a political point, for example attack an opponent
- give an incomplete answer
- repeat a previous answer
- claim to have answered the question already.

These findings come from research carried out by Dr Peter Bull and Kate Mayer of York University on television interviews given by Mrs Thatcher and Neil Kinnock during the 1987 general election. They also logged Mrs Thatcher's comments when interviewers tried to ask another question. These included:

- 'No, please let me go on'
- 'May I just finish'
- 'One moment'
- 'I must beg of you'
- 'Please may I'
- 'Let me finish it'
- 'Can I just finish it'
- 'Will you give me time'
- 'May I say something else'
- 'May I now and then say a word in my own defence'
- 'Please may I say'
- 'But can I just go on'
- 'Yes but one moment'
- 'Please, there's just one other thing'
- 'One moment, hold on'
- 'No, don't stop me'.

Old? Yes. Still valid? Assuredly. If politicians use these tactics on television against formidable interviewers, imagine how they carry on with novice print interviewers.

The point is that politicians increasingly wish to get their message across to the voters unhampered, unexamined, unquestioned. But the public don't read their manifestos – alas, many journalists don't either. So because politicians need the publicity afforded by political interviews, they have turned interviews into political rants and they bulldoze, they steamroller.

Journalists must remember that bulldozers can't cope with hilly terrain, they get stuck at the foot of deep valleys, they sink into mud.

LOCAL GOVERNMENT

Local politicians representing the largest and most powerful cities and counties can be every bit as tricky as MPs. Indeed, many MPs start in local government. Local politicians representing the smaller counties, cities and boroughs may have more limited back-up facilities but can be formidable too. For novice reporters, the best ones to interview are the newly elected who have almost everything to learn.

Though local politicians' status may be lower, the need for journalists to be accurate is as great; and so is the irritation experienced by misquoted local politicians. This is primarily because they live and work so close to their voters, whereas many Westminster MPs can trudge round their constituencies unrecognised.

If anything, the local loyalty factor is greater. MPs are more likely to kiss and make up with a local paper's political reporter who's annoyed them for two reasons. First, because sooner or later politicians need votes – and voters live locally. Second, because they are the best conduit available. On a national there are always other writers to approach.

Gain their trust

The advice for the journalist is: work the phones, attend the meetings, frequent the pubs, talk to the politicians, gain their trust. Jake Arnold-Forster, former editor of *Local Government Chronicle*, knows why he gets scoops. He gets on the phone and keeps phoning: councillors, chief executives, city people, national politicians: 'They're the ones who give you the rich returns.'

An outstanding local government reporter on the Southampton *Evening Echo* who went on to work for PA, was famous for spending 90 per cent of his time just talking to local politicians. 'He was on such good terms with them that, even if he wrote a story they found offensive, he could still go back the next day and talk to them about it, because they knew they could rely on him as a reporter,' says Bill Browne, former *Evening Echo* news editor, and now editor of the Basingstoke *Gazette*. 'Provided you can be seen to be fair and balanced, politicians will trust you.'

Local government reporting, he says, is often a trade-off: swopping one piece of news for another. 'Probably 60 to 70 per cent of what you learn doesn't make it into the story but may prove very useful later.' Browne says politicians are there to answer the difficult questions and so 'you ought to test them to the limit, making no allowances'. Sometimes this causes shock waves to run through elected councils, particularly the smaller ones at the very bottom of the statutory hierarchy: town and parish councils. Browne says:

> 'In Winchester, we reported on parish councils never touched before. When people see what they have said at meetings faithfully reported in their local newspaper it comes as one hell of a shock – but it's a great check on democracy. Otherwise a council can become a cosy club.'

Why do journalists sit through long meetings to the very end, listening to quite a few people in love with the sound of their own voices? Because power tends to corrupt and reporting what politicians say and do is one way to hold them to account and make them realise their power is vested in them by voters.

Local government officials

On the other side of local government are the officials – a mixed group. Some are stars in their own right, some tediously self-important, many of them delighted to be interviewed and talk about their work. The only given is do your research first and check how much respect they feel they need to be accorded.

A long-time freelance told me she'd only once had to interview as 'Silly Little Me privileged to talk to Knowledgeable You' and that was with a south London borough official. The interview related to catering outlets in the area and she says the interview went along the following lines:

> Freelance (after the usual preliminaries): 'I'm writing a feature about
> . . . and it seems to me [trotting out her research findings]. Am I right
> that . . .?'
> Official: 'Wrong. Rubbish.'
> Freelance: 'Well . . .'
> Official: 'You're like all journalists, think you know everything.'
> Freelance: 'No, I don't. That's why I'm here so . . .'
> Official: 'You know absolutely nothing. I've met people like you before.
> Come in here, thinking you know everything when you know nothing.

I've spent . . . years in local government, man and boy, and I know every inch of the borough. This is your first visit here, isn't it?' [It wasn't but I let it go.]

Freelance (alerted by the 'man and boy' clue): 'Mr . . ., that's why I'm here. To get the facts right. To talk to someone who knows all about it, so I don't make any stupid mistakes. I'd really appreciate as much help as you can give me. I know how important it is to get the facts from an expert.'

Official (slightly mollified): 'Well, at least you've come to the right person. I know what you need to know, so you'd better listen.'

And she did. 'I played up to it though I hated it. I'd like to report that he was awful, but the truth is that, with his ego massaged by dollops of wow and gosh and my goodness, he gave me a good interview.'

Hunting as a pack

All too often at press conferences journalists concentrate on the questions they want to ask or the questions the news desk has told them to ask and ignore one of the great interviewing guidelines: listen to the answers.

When journalists do listen and are able to ask follow-up questions, they get a better story. And when they decide to hunt in a pack, the result can be devastating. Harold Frayman of the *Observer* remembers a Conservative Party Central Office general election press conference with Mrs Thatcher, an acknowledged expert at not answering the question. 'General election press conferences are very formal set pieces,' says Frayman, 'and they have to finish at a set time.' This is because the next party press conference which the political journalists plan to attend is scheduled to begin x minutes later and timing is vital for journalists to meet deadlines.

'Tony Bevins at the *Express*, later at the *Mail*, asked a question that Mrs Thatcher really did not want to answer. She smiled and said "That's a very interesting question," and turned to another journalist and said "Bill . . .?"

Usually everyone's got questions they want to ask on their own account, and this would have worked most times, but on this occasion Bill said, "Actually, the question I would most like answered is the one Tony just asked you."

Mrs Thatcher grinned and said "Don't be silly," then turned to someone else and that someone else said, "Ah, yes. Now what I'd like to ask you is the question Tony asked." And for once – and it really was a once – the press pack ganged up instead of fighting individually and the truth was that it worked. She had to answer the question. She couldn't keep on turning it aside. Most press conferences go the way of the person running it. If there were more working together in press conferences there'd be more chance of getting answers.'

Working together like this is so rare that, when it happens, journalists present recollect it years later in their memoirs. At least 30 years after the event, Alistair Cooke in *Six Men* graphically recalled how American presidential hopeful Henry Wallace was asked whether he'd written a series of rather strange letters obtained by an opponent (Westbrook Pegler) and printed in a hostile publication over Wallace's signature. Wallace answered that he 'never discussed Westbrook Pegler'. He was asked four more times – once by Pegler – and made the same reply.

Then the famous journalist H. L. Mencken – the P. J. O'Rourke of his time – asked Wallace: 'Would you consider me a Pegler stooge?' After the laughter subsided, Wallace replied, 'No, Mr Mencken, I would never consider you anybody's stooge.' So Mencken continued:

> 'Well, then, it's a simple question. We've all written love letters in our youth that bring a blush later on. There's no shame in it. This is a question that all of us here would like to have answered, so we can move on to weightier things.'

Wallace made no answer, leaving listeners, as Cooke concludes, to draw the obvious conclusion.

Frayman points up another failure at press conferences: 'Journalists don't ask supplementaries when they could.' He remembers a reporter from one of the East Berlin newspapers asking Mrs Thatcher a question in the 1979 general election about her plans for the trade unions:

> '"But surely if you implement your plans to cut benefits you will end up with rioting on the streets?" Everybody laughed and she loudest of all. He turned up in 1983 to say "Given there has been rioting in the streets . . ." She was embarrassed by it but no one was prepared to take it up and run with it.'

Some reporters use a press conference to get an answer a politician might prefer not to give face to face or might wish later to deny. As Frayman says:

> 'They think they can get away with it one-to-one but not with 30 people there who have it in their notebooks. These comments are hostages to fortune. They know what they say may come back to haunt them.'

Poacher turned gamekeeper Robin Corbett knows the tricks of both trades. He handles press conferences when he wants to be quoted by offering the press sound-bites. 'You don't need to tip a million words over people. I say it all in three sentences and shut up.' And he makes sure he speaks vividly and in pictures.

The converse of this is true – and here's where knowing your quarry is so essential – when politicians *don't* want to be quoted they talk at great length, in a dreary, monotonous voice and waffle or ramble on. That's when concentrated listening becomes even more important.

10
Different interviewees
Celebrities

The bigger the star, the more constraints on the journalist. Here's Harrison Ford setting out his agenda.

> 'I'm here to transfer information. I'm here for no other reason than to bring this film to the public's attention. Actors and journalists have a symbiotic relationship. I'm here to serve you as long as you're here to serve me. I'm not here to become famous, I'm not here to have myths made about me. I'm here to help define your understanding of what I do and why I do it, which may have something new to offer people who have spent 20 years listening to the same crap.'

You can do this if you're world No. 1. On the journalist's part, the greater the need then for that magic interviewing ingredient confidence, reinforced with high-level powers of interest, enthusiasm, persuasion and/or effrontery (see pp. 117–26).

For the rest, it's all the basics but more so. More research, more sitting in their skin so you can understand what will encourage them to talk, more concentration and all to enable you to interview people with more experience and usually more to lose. Ask yourself how you would like to be frozen in print by a journalist with God knows what agenda.

Make requests for the celebrity interview with care. Present yourself and your publication as favourably as possible and work out why it should be in their interest to talk to you.

Use all your senses

Follow up any initial phone call with a letter and cuttings and be prepared to invest a lot of time and effort. Be persistent, persuasive and charming. Prepare well and from the moment you meet them use all your senses.

> Michael Crichton stretches his lofty frame back in the seat, hands clasped behind his head, the lines behind his eyes deepen as he considers the

matter in hand. Silence. He shifts position so that the fingers of his left hand are obscuring part of his face. More silence.

Surely the question is not that difficult: what has all your power and money bought you? Finally the man who is said to be America's highest-paid writer answers, though not before contemplating a paper cup containing ridiculously sweet coffee: 'It allows me to be resented wherever I go.'

(Michael Ellison, *Guardian*, 17 November 1999)

You have to absorb surroundings.

The room is filled with nasty brown chairs and teetering piles of paper. Shea's jolly red tie is the only colourful object in the Nato compound. Though he says he is not affected by stress, his shoulders are still up alongside his ears, their customary position during his famous briefings . . .

(Harriet Lane on Jamie Shea, Nato spokesman,
Observer, 5 March 2000)

You have to watch gestures and contrast what you've been told and what you see.

The next thing that strikes me is that he is quite peculiarly, unexpectedly nervous; he keeps writhing in his chair and squeezing his arms down between his legs – not at all the bland, sunny soul he appears on television. He keeps saying this is because he is shy of interviews, but he is not exactly new to the sport, nor did I have to twist his arm to get him. On the contrary, when I had to cancel my appointment, it was he who rang the next day to set a new date.

(Lynn Barber on Melvyn Bragg,
Independent, 17 June 1990)

Nowhere in this book will you find praise for journalists who write more about themselves than the people they interview. Egomaniac interviewers are really ill-disguised columnists with insufficient material and so rarely last long. Writing about yourself is easy, no research required, but there is a catch. You need to be interesting. Witness this intro:

I arrive at Sir Edward Heath's house in Salisbury with a gift for him. I didn't mean to bring him a gift. It's just that I was early and had wandered into the high street to kill half an hour and there, in a shop window, was a tie covered in bright, multi-coloured yachts. He'll like that, I thought. He'll be charmed by it. Plus he'll think I'm a very nice person to have bought him such a gift. He won't be his usual, famously grumpy and abrupt self . . .

And on and on – a bad compass error at the start of an interview clearly heading for the rocks.

CELEBRITY INTERVIEWERS

Of the interviewers who deserve to be taken seriously, there are two sorts: those who interview celebrities and those who are 'celebrity interviewers'. Lynda Lee-Potter (see p. 126) is one of the first, Andrew Duncan (p. 117) and Lynn Barber two of the second.

Perceptive, witty and unafraid, Barber puts the case for celebrity interviewing better than anyone else. Read her books *Mostly Men* and *Demon Barber*, particularly the forewords. She admits she admires people who have the drive to become famous and is very curious about the effect fame has on people, but she *never interviews from the knees*. Far from it. She knows you can't be a fan and an interviewer at the same time.

She writes in the first person, finding it like 'a leap from darkness into light'. She discovered that when not 'encumbered with this terrible overcoat of objectivity and omniscience' she could say what actually happened. She may write about herself but she never loses sight of her interviewee.

When you interview celebrities, her advice is: do your homework and go in well prepared and very curious. Demonstrate early on, through a highly informed question, that you know a great deal about them, signalling that you expect them to make an effort too. The best question is the shortest one that will unlock the longest answer, she says. Either start nice and turn nasty, or start nasty and turn nice. She uses tape recorders.

Because most celebrities are plugging something, she lets them plug it early and often at length, listening carefully for their turn of phrase, pitch and speed of speaking. This means she can later pick up any tell-tale hesitation or glibness.

She knows that tough questioning usually produces good quotes. By contrast with the *Sunday Times* interviewer who asked Harriet Harman 'Would you call yourself an intellectual?', Barber asked 'Are you thick?' She knows that when people have to defend themselves to someone they find genuinely interested in them, they often produce passionate and printable answers.

She said about her 'thick' question that it 'sounds ruder'. Correct, but I would bet she asked it in a way that didn't give offence. She knows that the really deadly questions are the dulcet ones. I'm also sure she never asked the thick question until she was certain Harman knew how very interested Barber was in what Harman had to say.

Barber says she's a better interviewer now at 40+ than she was when young and pretty. On flirting she says:

'You don't *need* sexual chemistry, when the chemistry of taking an intense, informed interest in someone is so potent. There are very few people in the world who can resist the opportunity to talk about themselves at length to someone who seems genuinely, deeply interested and who has obviously thought about (i.e. read up) their life beforehand.'

Hunter Davies, by contrast, uses a notebook, stays a maximum of two hours and, like everyone with any sense, wants to see people at home. He goes in with topics rather than questions and says he starts soft and soppy. Like Lynn Barber he prefers to ask about a celebrity's childhood, since he says it's a truth not universally acknowledged that all famous people are the same.

He admits to one trick: he starts discussing the interview with them after he's closed his notebook, asking why they gave certain answers. He belongs to the low cunning group, saying curiosity, empathy and fluttering eyelashes are not enough.

He also shows people what he's written before it's published, allowing them to correct factual mistakes. He says he doesn't know any other interviewer who does this. That sentence should read 'who admits to doing this' since many journalists on nationals as well as weeklies and magazines do it – but don't let on.

The art of seduction

Suzie Mackenzie of the *Guardian* calls interviewing 'the art of practised seduction' and admits to using every wile.

'You're going to smile, to laugh at their jokes, give them every possible sign that they have your complete attention – that, when they look into your eyes, the person you are seeing is the person they want you to see. But interviewing is not about charming someone, it's to do with making them want to charm you and then not resisting their charm.'

Andrew Billen in the *Evening Standard* knows how much interviewers can be deceived. 'The one time I subsequently had a proper relationship with one of my subjects, I discovered that almost everything she had told me on the record had contained a lie of commission or omission.'

We may all have an immutable inner core, but we all respond differently to different people – so interviews are necessarily snapshots in time. To think one can capture or even approach a person's essence in an hour-long interview is wishful, not to say self-deluding.

Billen, too, sees the similarity between celebrity interviewing and seduction, and admits to worrying much more about the potential two-facedness of interviewers. 'Once you've said goodbye there's no professional obligation to maintain in print the sympathetic smile with which you received an indiscretion.' You can twist, editorialise, boost, belittle. Like Lynn Barber he justifies his decisions by saying if there is any honour in interviewing, it must lie in the relationship between interviewer and the reader. 'When someone asks me what so-and-so was really like, I always reply that I have tried to answer exactly that question in my piece.'

The cynical view is that a typical showbiz interview is like a rendezvous with a hooker. Xan Brooks in *Big Issue* writes:

> You meet in an anonymous hotel room. You have an allotted time together. All too often the interviewee doesn't know who you are or where you come from. The subject provides basic information (well-worn anecdotes passed off as revelation) while the questioner fishes pathetically for something more deep and lasting.

The bigger the star, the more difficult the interview can be. The converse is true: those seeking fame will often trade personal secrets for publicity and rarely complain.

Barry Norman, showbiz writer for the *Daily Mail* before turning to television, says it's very important to put stars at ease and that's often more difficult than it might sound.

> 'Movie stars usually have a kind of tunnel vision – which is understandable. They're in a precarious position because there are always people younger and prettier and probably better actors – movie stardom and acting rarely go together – coming along behind them.'

One approach, he says, is to start by asking 'How did this film come about? What's your involvement?' Then, you know you'll get something you can use. 'It might not be terribly fascinating but it's a good icebreaker and gets them talking.'

British actors are easier to interview than Hollywood stars, Norman says.

> 'Very few of them get huge money and they've usually had to struggle. Overnight success for the average British actor takes ten years and they remember it. They remember when they were poor, scurrying round trying to find another small speaking part in a TV play.
> Big movie stars forget quickly that they were once poor. They're surrounded with bodyguards and it makes them feel important. Their entourage are telling them all the time how marvellous, how wonderful they are, and they believe it.'

As far as ploys go, Norman knows the power of silence.

> 'If a guy has told you something which he knows is not the whole truth, or only part of the truth, and you sit there and look at him and let five or ten seconds go by, he will almost certainly start explaining further and

you're getting close to the kind of stuff you really want. But it takes some nerve. Don't be afraid.'

He's alert to counter-ploys. 'When they start using little tricks you know it's because they are trying to evade the real issue.' Take leg crossing. 'If an attractive woman is doing it, it may mean she's trying to distract your attention from what you're asking. "Hang on" you think, "there's something in these questions she doesn't want to talk about."'

Norman's rule is to interview only those stars, writers and directors whose work he likes. 'I don't see any point in giving free publicity to rubbish.' But some interviewers do, and some make celebrities look foolish. Occasionally the celebrities strike back with deadly effect, as when Germaine Greer wrote about her experience with an unnamed 'celebrity interviewer' so devastatingly that Lynn Barber, for instance, went into print saying it wasn't her. Catherine Deneuve did the same, less vituperatively on Sally Vincent; so too Willem Dafoe's agent a *Guardian* writer. Beware.

For more cautionary stories, see appendices 1 and 2. First, the celebrity interview parodied in Q&A format by Miles Kington; second, an interview with Madonna, also in Q&A format, showing what is lost (and found) in translation.

INTERVIEWER PROFILE: ANDREW DUNCAN

Andrew Duncan's *Radio Times* interviews make national headlines. That alone would mark him out as exceptional. He is more: an interviewing phenomenon. A strategist, tactician, joker, supremely and rightly confident in his talent.

He does not belong to that wearisome group of egomaniac journalists who appear to interview by looking in a mirror. He interviews celebrities, concentrating on them. He doesn't efface himself – a flavour of the man is there in his copy – but the 'I' count in his interviews is minimal. All this, plus an elegant, ironic style.

So why is he so good? Because he's a sympathetic listener, he says. If only it were that simple. Because he genuinely finds people interesting, he adds. A lot of us do, yet . . . Because he once sold encyclopedias on commission in Toronto – most certainly. Also because he's disarming and assured at the same time. He gets seasoned, suspicious interviewees to drop their defences and he's always in control, though not all his interviewees realise it.

First, a health warning for novice interviewers. Andrew Duncan is a very experienced journalist. He's perfected his interviewing technique after years of practice. You should do the same.

Mrs Thatcher

Duncan is generous, almost profligate, in talking about past interviews and his approach to interviewing. He drops names throughout: Prince Edward, Robert Redford, Elton John, Arthur Miller, Demi Moore, the Spice Girls, Dolly Parton. But there's just one place to start. His headline-making interview with Mrs Thatcher. As always, he'd asked for and had been given an hour.

> 'I was told I couldn't discuss her time in power or her book, bought by the *Sunday Times*. So what on earth was the point of going to see her?
> I said, "How nice to see you again. How's everything?" We chatted and after about 10 minutes I said, "That's it." I started to pack up and prepare to leave and naturally Mrs Thatcher was surprised. "Well," I said, "I'm really sorry about this but I can't ask you about your time in office and I can't ask you about the book and the only questions I've got are rude ones."
> "Oh," she said, "We *love* rude questions."
> "Really?" I said. "Why do you drink so much whisky?"
> "What do you mean?"
> I said, "Alan Clark's diaries, page 67."'

And away they went. Her sidekick began to look nervous, Duncan says, but the interview flowed on. He questioned her about relations with her son Mark and then the fact that there was no mention of her mother in her *Who's Who* entry. Duncan recalls: 'I'd taken the precaution of looking in *Who's Who*, then remembered my edition was two years old. When she queried it I said, "I looked it up this morning." To which she replied, "Oh, then we must do something about that."' He put it in the *Radio Times* interview and the quote made headlines in every national UK paper. Not only then, he adds, but also on the anniversary, when she still had not put her mother into *Who's Who*.

So the lessons here are clear. He understood his quarry:

> 'Mrs Thatcher had an hour set aside. She programmes herself totally. An hour for this, an hour for that. When it looked as though the interview might end after 10 minutes, she had a three-quarter hour yawning gap with nothing to do, so she had to continue and she did. It was a trap. I thought the odds were in my favour but of course she could have said, "Thank you very much. That's fine."'

Good research in evidence, too. It's well known that politicians faced with a statement which they think may be based on rumour or guesswork demand substantiation.

> 'People say you . . .'
> 'Exactly who says so?'

Certainly the information about Mrs Thatcher drinking whisky came from Alan Clark's diaries and sounded good and convincing, whether Duncan quoted the right page or not.

Preparation

Having glimpsed Duncan's style, let's go sequentially through his interviewing process, starting with setting up the interview. This is normally arranged by *Radio Times*. He always asks for an hour alone with the interviewee. PRs are forbidden, unless the circumstances are exceptional (royals, for instance).

And the location? Over a good lunch in a good restaurant, which helps his interviewees relax. New York, LA, Rome, Paris suit him well. If the interview is to be in London, he has his own table at the Caprice. He always orders champagne, because it makes the occasion festive. Not surprisingly, he avoids the BBC canteen and dislikes interieving on the set.

Research? 'I do a huge amount. I get all the cuttings.' They're couriered or emailed to him. He normally has a list of 60 questions in his head and says he usually gets through 40 to 60 of them. 'I get really cross if I haven't done them in an hour.' He makes it his business to discover some recondite piece of information that they wouldn't expect him to know. 'I bring this in at a very early stage. They say, "How do you know that?"' This signals to them not to try any wool-pulling. You will always get programmed answers at the start, he says, but he tries to get rid of them in the first few minutes. More of that featuring repetitive Robert Redford later.

Duncan says: 'Far too many celebrities have contempt for journalists and that's quite disturbing, although I think they're right. So many journalists don't do their homework or have the courtesy to know what the guy they're interviewing has done.'

His preparation does not include changing his clothes to match his interviewee's.

> 'My absolute fundamental is always wear a suit. I thought with Noel Gallagher if I dress down it will look as if I'm trying too hard, like parents of teenagers trying to be teenagers. But I realised I had to explain, so I said "I'm very sorry but I'm going to see the Inland Revenue." "I thought you were the Inland Revenue," he said.'

In the south of France, though, he did wear shorts when interviewing Robbie Williams. His alleged girlfriend at the time, Geri Halliwell, would have expected no less, Duncan says.

Some interviewers take presents as softeners. Duncan doesn't. He says he once took champagne to Murray Walker, who was giving him lunch at his home, but Walker 'put it in the fridge and offered me a glass of orange juice, cup of tea, something like that.'

Demi Moore

Duncan establishes rapport easily. 'If it's a girl I flirt away and if it's a man I might try to be conspiratorial. I always smile and treat it as a joke, however grand they are.' However, a tougher side of him emerges if PRs try to sit in. He met Demi Moore – 'insecure but looks great' – and her PR for an agreed hour-long interview but the PR said '40 minutes' and made the mistake of sitting down.

> 'I said: "If you're sitting here, what I've got is no minutes, because I'm actually not going to do the interview if you're sitting here. I never do and I'm not going to start now. If Demi can't look after herself with a humble interviewer like myself then it's too bad. I'm not going to rape her or anything like that. I'm not going to interview with you here. It makes it not real. It won't do her any good. Goodbye." Exit PR.
>
> "I think this is going to be a really enjoyable experience," Demi said.
>
> "I'll try and make it that way," I said. After half-an-hour the PR returns and says "That's it."
>
> "What do you mean, 'that's it'? I've only had 30 minutes."
>
> "That's it. One more question."
>
> "OK, one more question. I'm sorry about this but have you ever had plastic surgery?"
>
> "I don't believe you're asking me that," Demi said.
>
> "Why not?"
>
> "Do you want to know how I wipe my bottom, back to front or front to back?"
>
> "Well, if you want to tell me – but it won't go in the piece."
>
> "I cannot believe you're asking me this."
>
> "Well, the reason is *St Elmo's Fire* and *Striptease*. There's a difference between them. I would have put it more gracefully . . ."
>
> Demi gets up. She's shouting. She says "I just can't believe it." I said, "I take it that's a 'Yes'." She walked out and cancelled the whole of her European tour. It took, I think, five hours before she calmed down and agreed to do a few more interviews, with the PR sitting there.'

Every subsequent interview mentioned plastic surgery. He concludes: 'It's a dialogue – on my terms.'

Michael Palin

The Demi Moore interview was untypical – mostly they're very good-humoured. Duncan uses a digital, state-of-the-art recorder, setting it up very matter-of-factly on the table. With a much-interviewed celebrity he may begin with a disclaimer. 'Let's start by agreeing that everything that's been printed about you is rubbish and this'll probably be more lies, so let's just have a nice lunch.' This gets them on your side, he says.

He never appears, please note the word *appears*, to take the interview too seriously. Sometimes he says: 'Don't worry about a thing. I've written it already, and this is just a performance.' He's a very sympathetic listener and laughs and smiles a lot. 'I want people to think of me as a mate, someone who doesn't give a stuff, only asking these questions because he can't think of anything else.'

He keeps an unobtrusive eye on the recorder and has only once had it fail. This was when he was interviewing Michael Palin.

> 'He spoke very movingly for the first time about his sister's suicide. Fantastic and I thought "God, you're clever, Andrew." I kept looking at my recorder, checking it was going round, doing all the things it should do.
>
> I got back and was going to transcribe it and it was blank. What I'd done, I think, was put the microphone into the earpiece, so it still showed it was playing. In a total panic I phoned the manufacturers. "Is there any way, however much it costs, to retrieve it?" They said no.'

He was too ashamed to tell Palin the truth at the time, though he told him later, so concocted some story about the recorder being stolen. They repeated the interview but, as to be expected, it wasn't so good. The upshot, says Duncan, is that now he's terrified and checks all the time, carrying a pair of earphones with him.

Never disagree

So where does selling encyclopedias in Toronto come in? Duncan says:

> 'The best training. It's sheer hell. You're dropped off in the morning in some small town or village and left there. What you learn is that you never, ever, disagree with anyone. If they say it's too expensive you say "Absolutely. I quite agree."'

This patently is not an inviolable rule, vide Demi Moore, but one he uses frequently. 'Disagreeing is a terrible mistake,' he says, 'because it puts their hackles up.'

He once offended Burt Reynolds by admitting he'd read a book by one of his former wives.

> 'He was furious, so rather than argue I said, "I'm very sorry. I didn't mean to offend you. I'm very very sorry, now let's move on." When you're asking a difficult question, you must always have another question in mind, a back-up to defuse the situation. If they get cross, you just smile and ignore it.'

He's very good at reading people, so if he knows there's a subject they don't want to talk about, he'll adopt one of several approaches depending on their character. Perhaps he'll studiously avoid all mention, approaching very near it but veering off at the last moment. This he did with film director Roman Polanski, who hates journalists.

> 'I thought, I won't mention the rape conviction which prevents him returning to the US because at some stage *he* will. Then I will say, "I wasn't going to mention that but as you have . . .'
> "Will you ever go back to America?", I asked.
> "No, I don't think so because people like you would bring all that stuff up."
> "What stuff?"
> "Well, that stuff . . ."
> "I wasn't going to mention it, so why would you say I'd bring it up? I'm not interested in being a voyeur 30 years on . . ."
> I went back to his being 67 and having an 18-month-old child.'

And in the end, of course, they discussed the rape case.

Duncan used a variation of this technique on Harrison Ford, in his intro.

> 'Here is the agreement – I promise not to mention the C word [carpenter] to the Star of the Century if he tries not to be the boring "terrible interview" he claims to be.
> He smiles. "I'm quite good really, but on my terms – that we discuss the work, and you ask fascinating questions." '

In the end, of course, they got round to the C word.

If he's forbidden to mention a particular subject, he declines the interview. Duncan says he'll ask what he likes and the subject is quite entitled to tell him to mind his own business. Sometimes this backfires. Actress Robin Givens, formerly Mrs Mike Tyson, said she wouldn't answer questions about the boxer. 'Is it true that he beat you?' Duncan asked. Givens turned off his tape recorder and walked out.

Prince Edward

Duncan designs his questions to get quotes. A PR was in attendance when he interviewed Prince Edward – 'some young girl from a TV station' – but he silenced her by warning that, 'If you say one word I'll get up and walk out and put that in the article.'

Talking to Prince Edward about the monarchy and Britain he said:

> 'We're told there is a rigid class system but it's a load of codswallop. I don't believe there's a class system, do you?'
> 'You're quite right,' said Prince Edward. 'There is no class system.'

Headlines, headlines, headlines. Sometimes people have to be drawn into admitting what they really think, he says.

Fay Weldon

Duncan knew that playwright and novelist Fay Weldon had fallen out with the sisterhood and when he interviewed her got her talking about rape – asking whether date rape is the same as a man raping an under-age girl. 'She went over the top, saying rape isn't the worst thing that can happen to a woman.' Knowing what a reaction that would provoke, he faxed her the paragraph he had written, asking 'Did you actually mean this?' She faxed back saying 'I will defend this to the death.'

As soon as the interview appeared, there was outrage and Weldon denied she'd said it but Duncan had the tape and the fax.

> 'If somebody tells me something in confidence, I usually try and talk them out of it. "Well, I won't say that but I could say . . ." You're trying to get people to tell you things they wouldn't normally say and if it's going to hurt them you shouldn't do it but . . .'

The sentence comes to a stop. He sent Fay Weldon a case of champagne afterwards.

Robert Redford

Duncan hates news management with the fierceness of a journalist who has seen the noose tighten. Marvel at this intro:

> The second floor of the exclusive Crillon Hotel in Paris is agog with self-importance. Thigh-booted girls, impossibly tall and gloatingly gorgeous, do important things with mobile telephones; haughty, frock-coated waiters glide by with trays of tea; a film crew, latched electronically together, perspires on the stairs; a trio of middle-aged women smoke furiously in a state of post-interview *tristesse*; a girl sits at a desk cluttered with lists, name tags and folders of information; another clicks a button on her stopwatch, groans and ushers a group into the presence of the 'talent'. I flick through instructions of where his photographs must be retouched . . . 'the wrinkled area between his lower lip and chin', 'the veins on his nose', 'the area around the neck and throat', 'soften the forehead lines'.
>
> Oh artifice, thy name is a superstar interview. There are far fewer fol-de-rols in meeting a president, a prime minister, a royal. Yet such is Robert Redford's practised charm and, it seems, genuine modesty, that all frustrations disappear on meeting.
>
> (*Radio Times*, 18 February 1995)

Duncan remembers how during the interview he'd ask Redford a question and

> 'He'd answer with a quote I'd read in the *New York Times* about a totally
> different question. Like, "I was in Paris in the early days and before I
> answer this question I just want to tell you how much I love Paris." I said
> "I've read this in connection with another question. What I asked you
> was. . . ."'

The 'Arthur Miller quote'

The ploy he finds most effective for many celebrities, particularly those who
have got to hide their mixed-up backgrounds, is what he calls the Arthur
Miller quote.

> 'This still slays them. It goes this way: "I was talking to Arthur Miller
> yesterday or the day before and he said to be really creative you have got
> to have a fairly dysfunctional background. That really helps. Do you think
> that's true?"
> They've heard of Arthur Miller and say, "Oh my God, yes."'

Duncan admits to a lot of name-dropping and says sometimes he feels nause-
ated when he listens to the tape. 'I'm hideously creepy.'

He immerses himself in the cuttings but scorns using other people's material.
'It's got to be fresh. It can't be a cuttings job.' That's why he gets nervous
before his interviews. He has to get all his material then and there.

Elton John

Duncan says the only time he ever used a cuttings quote was with Elton John,
because he didn't have the time to prepare properly for the interview, thinking
Elton would cancel on him. He acknowledges that he had been rather preju-
diced against 'the lachrymose pudding'.

Knowing that Elton admired Versace, he arrived for the interview wearing a
Versace tie and managed to let one of Elton's CDs fall out of the bag he was
carrying. He didn't expect to like Elton but he did. They both have houses
in the south of France, so common ground was established fairly quickly and
it moved the interview on to a totally different level. 'He was brilliant. I liked
him, I really liked him.'

John Major

Duncan's least favourite but curiously most quote-worthy interviewees are
sports people, tennis players in particular, but he enjoys politicians because

they're used to being asked questions – though not the sort he asks. 'It's only in this job that you talk to people about subjects so intimate that your parents or your best friend wouldn't discuss with you. You get to ask questions which are terribly personal, cheeky and offensive.'

Such questions provoke a response from most people but politicians are tougher meat.

> 'For instance, with John Major, to put him on the spot I asked, "Isn't it a bit offensive to have your son's wedding pictures appear in a tacky magazine like *Hello!?*" Unfortunately, it didn't work because Major said, "I'm not discussing my children," and I said "Quite right."'

The best thing with politicians, says Duncan, is to make them feel sorry for you. 'If you can pretend complete ignorance they become terribly pompous and give away a side of themselves not always seen.' A caveat here – this approach may work in celebrity interviews but it is not for straightforward political interviews.

Spice Girls

One last glimpse of Duncan, gloriously in charge. A few years ago he was asked to interview the Spice Girls for the Christmas issue of *Radio Times*. They were about to release their film and were just beginning that slide from the height of their fame.

> 'I was told it would be in Rome on Tuesday and I'd have half an hour with them, on my own. I could just about do that. Then "it won't be Rome it will be Paris and there'll be two of you". What am I going to get? I thought.
>
> I went to Paris and saw the film and was told there'd be 40 journalists and we had 15 minutes. I thought "Sod this for a laugh". I was about 100 years older than anyone there, dressed in a suit like a bloody bank manager again, so I sat right at the front. These two PR girls came in and there were two people on each side with a microphone. They said you've got one question each and please don't do more than that.
>
> I took over the whole conference. I had to. There was no way I could have done it otherwise. I said "Why did you steal from Mandela? Do you think it's funny?" The PR girls kept saying "no" and the Danes [Duncan is no lover of Danish journalists' perception of what makes a pertinent question] kept asking about their hair, but I said "Hang on a minute, I haven't finished."
>
> The girls with the microphones didn't dare stop me because they were frightened. It might have become unpleasant – I looked as if I would cause trouble if I had to. It was wonderful. Then one of the Spice Girls – Ginger – said "I really like you."
>
> "You think I'm your granddad, don't you?"
>
> "This is fun," she said.'

Duncan concludes: 'You have to be in control. Otherwise it's no good.'

'Interviewing is a craft,' he says, 'an act – liking people and not appearing to take it too seriously. If you're really interested it comes across.' He says his age, 60, helps.

> 'I can interview anybody now. It's much more difficult for a younger person to interview an older person than for an older person to interview a younger person – unless you're a pretty girl with nice long legs interviewing an old roué. That would help but I'm not sure you'd get what you want in interviewing terms.'

Dolly Parton

Duncan sums up his interviews as 'writing ephemera about ephemera' – but it's wonderfully stylish ephemera, which entertain millions of his readers and him too.

> 'I'd read that Dolly Parton says "I can get any man I want with my tits". So for half an hour I looked her straight in the eye.
> "Is this a record?" I asked.
> "Sure is honey," she said. "Now have a good look" and she thrust them in my face. "Now we can relax."
> Who says it's hard work?'

INTERVIEWER PROFILE: LYNDA LEE-POTTER

Lynda Lee-Potter is famous for her *Daily Mail* column, her features and her interviews. She's an outstanding, all-round journalist, not just a columnist and feature writer but a reporter whose news stories have made the front page.

Her training as an actress – she appeared on the West End stage before she married – gave her an acute ear for dialogue. She can read unattributed quotes and know who said them, and read so-called quotes from people she's interviewed and know they are not the interviewee's words. More than that, she is intuitive, able to stand between two people at a party and know that they are having an affair.

The key to interviewing, she says, is to concentrate totally.

> 'When I'm interviewing, nothing else will get in the way. People talk about "Doctor Theatre" – actors will go on stage with a broken leg. Certainly when interviewing if you've got flu or pneumonia it goes completely. You concentrate so totally that you lose yourself and you lose your aches and pains. Wonderful therapy, because for that time nothing intrudes.
> My way is to speak as little as possible and keep my questions incredibly simple and brief. The best interview is when you get that invisible cord between the two of you. You want to make the person you are talking to

feel fascinating and the object of your whole being, which indeed they are.

Interviewing is a job you never, ever crack.'

In the shadows

Lee-Potter almost always wears black. 'It happens subconsciously actually. You're not the star. And it works. I've often seen people several times over the years and they very rarely remember me.' This is a recognised sign of a great interviewer, though not recognised enough by beginners and the bombastic. Lee-Potter interviews celebrities but shuns being a 'celebrity interviewer'. 'I'm in the shadows,' she says. 'That's the way I prefer it.'

Preparation

She does as much preparation as possible: reads all the cuttings, biogs, finds out as much as possible about the person she's to interview. 'There's nothing worse than going to see somebody and asking an incredibly naff question about something you should know.'

She was interviewing the playwright John Mortimer (before he was knighted), and as she was coming out of the room heard the woman who was going in say: 'Now Mr Mortimer, tell me all about yourself.' A killer question, she says.

In an ideal world she'd always want at least two hours for the interview at the interviewee's house. Because she believes it's unforgivable to arrive late, she's always there hours early. 'I haven't the nerve to ring the doorbell two hours early so I'll park the car in a lay-by.' She uses the time rereading her research and looking over her questions so she goes in prepared. 'If you arrive late and flustered and forget the questions you want to ask, the first half hour will be wasted. There's no excuse for being late. You must allow time for things to go wrong.'

She says she's always terrified beforehand. 'My tummy turns over. I'm always anxious. Always. Always.' She may well ring the bell half an hour before the agreed time. 'I always say "I'm sorry I'm too early. Shall I go away?" Sometimes they'll say "Yes", sometimes "Come in".'

She starts the interview almost straightaway, having sussed out the room.

'When you walk in it's very important to case the joint and know where you're going to sit and where they're going to sit. If they show you into the drawing room and then go out, that's marvellous. If we're meeting in a restaurant, I have been known to move three times before the inter-viewee arrives. The killer situation is to be sitting opposite at a table or desk. It makes people rigid.'

She sets up two tape recorders, usually one either side of the table, 'because you never know if anything will go wrong' and she starts. Her method, she says, is to make people feel relaxed, warm, loved and at ease, beginning gently and concentrating on her interviewee completely. 'I work for a great editor, Paul Dacre, and he's got a million things on his mind, but when he's talking to you, you have his total and utter concentration.'

Fresh questions

Unless you're interviewing someone like Sir Peter Ustinov who, once prompted, can go into a monologue, then you and they are dependent on the questions, Lee-Potter says. She arrives with a list of questions, though depending on what her interviewees say, she may not ask them all. 'Listening is vital. They'll say something and you'll think, God, I must ask this. . . The more research you have done, the easier it is.'

Her questions are simple, brief and precise. 'If you ask fresh questions, you'll get a fresh interview. Don't ask hackneyed questions and you won't get hackneyed answers.'

That great interviewing gift – sensitivity – works for her. 'You've got to have an antenna, an instinct,' she says. 'You can sense things. Suddenly a question will come from nowhere and you don't know why you've asked it.' She matches her interviewing technique to her interviewee.

> 'In a way it's like being a psychiatrist. You've got to find the right way to ask. We're all different with different people. With the Commons hooker Pamella Bordes I discovered the only way to get her to tell you anything was to be really quite aggressive. Someone being aggressive to me would shut me up.'

Some interviewees ask 'What's your angle?' She tells them she hasn't got an angle.

> 'I just want to let them emerge as they are – boring, fascinating, tedious, witty or monsters – I mostly do it through quotes because I think people are revealed through what they say much more vividly than anything I might write. Everyone has a different way of writing. I rely on quotes tremendously.'

Living dangerously

As an interviewer, Lee-Potter has no recourse to tricks or deception but she admits that wine helps. It establishes a camaraderie, she says. Though she admits to being 'slightly in charge', she doesn't believe in being too controlling: 'I like to let the conversation gather its own momentum and sometimes let them take control. I'm all for "Let's live dangerously and see what happens".'

She's disliked very few of her interviewees, even if some of them are monsters. Sometimes the sweet ones will ask her questions, something she says just gets in the way.

> 'It's quite an art, deflecting personal questions about you in a way that doesn't sound rude or abrupt, but it must be done. Answer briefly and quickly go on to the next question. If you said you didn't want to talk, they'd think why and also feel irritated – they're talking about themselves, why shouldn't you?'

When things go wrong

'People's faces when they're being interviewed are incredibly revealing. You can see in their eyes when something goes wrong,' Lee-Potter says. 'You can see if they're cross or rattled. Sometimes, if they're rattled, it's important to press on. Again, it's an instinct to know when you have to withdraw instantly and change tack.'

There's a moment, she says, when they suddenly get bored. 'You can see it in their eyes and know they'll start repeating themselves. It's very important you spot that.' However, she rarely leaves until she's asked to. 'I stay to the bitter end. I can't think off-hand of any interview where I've gone of my own volition.'

When it comes to writing the interview up, quoting accurately is her passion.

> 'An approximation of what they say is not good enough. Everybody has an idiosyncratic way of talking and to get the meaning over without actually using the way they use words isn't good enough.
>
> Sometimes I'll read interviews with people I've interviewed and I'll know there's no way they'd ever have said that. They wouldn't use those words. They might express that meaning but not speak in that way. If you get what they say right, they're often happy with the interview. They're less likely to be happy if you get it wrong.'

Interview over

Bob Hope, says Lee-Potter, has had masses of mistresses.

> 'I went to interview his wife at the Ritz and was told that if I even mentioned a book written by one of his mistresses, his wife would terminate the interview.
>
> It was a dreadful interview. His wife just wouldn't say anything, all "wonderful man, happiest life ever". Absolute drivel, so I thought you have to go for broke and I said "——" whatever the book was called.

With great dignity she stood up and without a look at the entourage walked out. The entourage followed. Nobody said a word. I have no regrets because the interview wasn't going anywhere. It was worth the gamble and it gave me a funny item for my column.'

The one that got away

'I want to use everything,' Lee-Potter says, 'but if people say "Please don't use this, it's off the record" I would never use it.'

Some time ago she interviewed someone world-famous, who'd never been interviewed before but who agreed on condition he could see the copy. 'We had a wonderful lunch and he was completely open.' Too open it turned out.

'He said "It would break my heart if this ever appeared", so it never did. Of course I've kept my word. I see him at dinners occasionally and he always says hello. I write to him every year and ask can I come and interview you and he always writes back to say the answer is no. I've a very soft spot for him.'

Like all great interviewers, she likes the people she interviews. Over a long career she selects just three she'd rather not see again: Elaine Paige, Raquel Welch and Pamella Bordes. The first two were a pain, though she acknowledges she saw Elaine Paige at a difficult moment in her emotional life. Pamella Bordes 'I could have throttled'.

Lastly, says Lee-Potter, 'I'm uninsultable and I think that's a good quality. It doesn't matter what people say, it's all grist to the mill.'

Cardinal sins

- Taking your eyes off your interviewee.
- Thinking you have to be bold and daring and prove how clever you are by asking questions early on about subjects you've been warned against. Ask gently but not until the end of the interview.
- Interrupting people, particularly famous actors, in the middle of anecdotes, even if you've read the story in the cuttings several times. 'Fatal. You have got to let them tell it and then not use it.'
- 'If someone says "this is off the record," never try to double-cross them – because you only double-cross people once. They know, they remember, they tell their friends.'

11
Different interviewees
Special cases

Reluctant interviewees, inexperienced interviewees, business people, vulnerable people, children and the bereaved ('death knocks' and 'fatals' in newspaper jargon) need special handling, as do interviews where PRs sit in and 'two-handers', where it's the interviewers who double up.

RELUCTANT INTERVIEWEES

You have maybe two seconds before they slam the door on you. What can you do? Try stepping back. This is unexpected and, in a strange way, magnetic. As you step back they seem drawn forward.

If they don't shout at you to get off their property or slam the door in your face at this point, they'll probably agree to talk eventually. Say who you are and what you are doing, then there can be no mistake about why you are there, says experienced doorstepper Mike Biggs, formerly with Brennan's news agency at Heathrow.

Never park directly outside the house and certainly don't adopt an aggressive or eager tone of voice. The key is to make it clear that there's a need for their side of the story and you're offering them that opportunity. You say something like:

> 'People keep making these allegations and for your own protection you have to put your point of view.'

> 'How do you answer what . . . is saying?'

> 'It looks bad if you don't comment. We'd like to print your side of the story.'

Don't take offence however much they swear at you or whatever insults they pour on you or your paper. Stay cool and calm and continue to put it to them that what's being said about them should be answered and they are the ones best placed to do that.

Listen and sympathise

You can defuse their fury by listening. You don't have to agree with them in their rant – though that is often a great way to deflect anger – but you can soothe using sympathy.

> 'Lies, lies! – All bloody lies – ruining my life!'
> 'I can see that it must be a terrible worry for you and the family.'

> 'How would you like it if the bloody bitch said that about you?'
> 'I'd hate it – and I'd want to defend myself . . .'

> 'Why should I talk to you? You printed those vile allegations.'
> 'We can't print what we don't know. If what . . . says is false, tell me what really happened.'

Make it plain that talking to you will benefit them. You're there to help them clear their name. Never say any of the following:

> 'Come off it!'

> 'How could you?'

> 'That was stupid.'

> 'You didn't, surely?'

When to use your notebook

Keep your notebook in your pocket at first. The time to bring it out is after they've relaxed and invited you in, or when they've said something telling or incriminating that requires further comment.

> 'You said . . .'

Alternatively, use a pocket tape recorder with an unobtrusive mike or go straight back to the car and write down everything you can remember, timed and dated in your notebook.

If you suspect the interview is going to be tricky and/or dangerous, then take someone along as a witness, but warn them *not* to join in the questioning. You may be picking a delicate path that leads gently to a crucial question. The interviewee may hesitate, poised on the brink of a revealing answer, when the idiot with you, unused to pauses and the ways of interviewing, jumps in with a question that destroys your whole carefully constructed sequence.

Keep on asking the question you want answered. Rephrase it, walk round it, approach it from a variety of ways. Get to the nitty-gritty by persistence – and remember you are there for the readers, asking the questions they'd like answered.

INEXPERIENCED INTERVIEWEES

They may be wary or trusting, indiscreet or guarded, but all first-time inter-viewees are unused to dealing with the press, so don't foul it up for those who follow. An ordinary person interviewed just once in a lifetime by a journalist probably tells 30 other people about the experience and any poor practice just kicks us all further down the list of the trustworthy – and we're already rated below estate agents.

Inexperienced interviewees usually need the least cajoling of any to take part. Difficulties start with directions: this is where you must get the names of the roads rather than 'second on the left after the bridge' and repeat them back at least once. If you can persuade your interviewee to send/fax you a sketch map, so much the better. Always check where they will be immediately before the planned interview just in case you are delayed or have to cancel. Also, always ask for more time than usual, since the preliminaries often take up 10 to 15 minutes.

It's important when fixing the interview to give them a good but not too detailed idea of what you want to talk about. If you give too much warning you may get over-rehearsed answers, which lack vitality.

Easy does it

As ever, try to arrive in good time, but this is one occasion where your novelty value means that delays will be forgiven. Prepare to be looked over very quizzi-cally and to answer an assortment of questions about the publication, your job, other interviews you've done. Be human and agreeable. Smile. This is an occasion where being brisk and businesslike is a mistake, so don't be in a hurry.

Wipe your feet carefully and shed any soaked raincoat in the porch. Don't sit down until asked to do so and if you're offered tea or coffee, accept. Refusing appears rude and gets things off to a bad start. It also gives the interviewee a chance to exit to the kitchen and update the family about you. You'll be forgiven at the end if you haven't finished your drink – they will think it's because you found the interview so riveting.

Take your time to greet everyone in the room, including the cat or dog. Don't rush the preliminaries but when they're over, offer your interviewee a copy of the publication if appropriate, your card, and take out your notebook and/or tape recorder. Don't start though until your interviewee is settled.

Most inexperienced interviewees will be curious rather than apprehensive and will be looking forward to the interview, so make it a pleasant experience.

Explain again what you're after so they can collect their thoughts. If they appear nervous, then proceed calmly and gently. Verbal reassurance is often counter-productive, rather like saying to a child going to the dentist for the first time, 'Don't worry – it won't hurt!'

Start with a question you know they can answer with ease: a question on a safe subject. Get them talking before you approach any difficult or tricky areas. Depending on the subject of the interview, having more than one person in the room can help or hinder. If the interview is about some achievement or event, then input from others with anecdotes and colourful details can be very valuable.

If it's about relationships and/or traumas, then you must accept that sometimes what's said will be coloured by who else is in the room and may be said for their benefit rather than yours. This is tricky, and devising ways to get an interviewee on their own is difficult. Other people can be sent out to get more tea, locate photographs, etc. but it doesn't always work.

Fair warning

With inexperienced interviewees, you will almost always find yourself in complete control. It's a rare first-time interviewee who has worked out an agenda and answers accordingly. Most will do their best to be helpful and answer your questions fully, so these must be devised to bring out the story you're after. You'll find silence works wonderfully well here.

Your interviewee may be vulnerable because of lack of experience and you may have to decide whether to warn them not to be indiscreet. If you're told 'We bought this old picture because we wanted the frame for just £15 and then discovered it was an early Lord Leighton and sold it for £80,000', do you check with them they have declared capital gains tax, letting them know that the Inland Revenue reads magazines for just this sort of information? If they tell you in the course of recounting how they have triumphed over some tragedy just how much trouble they have encountered from thoughtless neighbours, do you ask them to think how this will look in print?

You have to realise that they may be beguiled by your attentive listening and encouraging comments into saying much, much more than they intended. It's OK if these techniques work on people in the public eye or with responsible jobs nominated by their firms to talk to the press, but is it fair for the inexperienced? You have to decide.

BUSINESS PEOPLE

The bigger the corporation, the more intensive and expensive media-training the executives will have received – almost certainly more than the journalists who interview them.

It's not just that for them time is money, though if a highly paid executive is going to give up an hour of his day to talk to a journalist there must be something in it for the corporation. It's that any company listed on a stock exchange is supposed in theory to give important information to the exchange and all its shareholders before telling anyone else.

From the company's viewpoint, executives need to know they should avoid any public comment that might move the company's share price up or down. Ken Gooding, former specialist writer for the *Financial Times*, explains,

> 'Corporations have just as much at stake as senior politicians when their executives are interviewed. An ill-judged, off-the-cuff remark from a senior executive can damage a company, as Gerald Ratner found when he jokingly described one of the products sold in his shops as "crap".'

Company executives, Gooding believes, also have more reason to be economical with the truth than politicians. 'When interviewing a business person you don't know well, it's best to ask yourself at frequent intervals, "Why is this lying bastard lying to me?"' But, he says, it's very important not to let these thoughts show. Most senior business people have large egos. 'Often that's what has driven them up the corporate ladder'. They're surrounded by staff who treat them deferentially – certainly not asking rude or mocking questions or making critical remarks.

It is possible, Gooding says, to ask difficult questions and still remain on friendly terms with your interviewee by making it clear the criticism has been levelled by someone else.

> 'You say, "One of your competitors suggests that there have been problems with that particular model and it is difficult to control at high speeds. Is there any truth in that?" rather than, "That model has a terrible reputation for swerving all over the place on motorways. What are you going to do about it?"'

Given what's at stake, it's no wonder that business people are so highly trained. During practice interviews they learn how to take control, how to make the points they want to make no matter what they're asked, and how to deal with possible 'difficult' questions.

No wonder, either, that PRs figure largely on corporate payrolls or that smaller companies employ outside consultants. The aim is to exert as much control over the press as possible. PRs advise on which journalists and publications to talk to, a selection often based on which can be trusted to be accurate.

PRs usually brief executives before the interview about the journalist – not just their CV but also about recent work and whether the journalist is likely to be 'friendly' to the company. Big corporations will almost certainly ask any journalist requesting an interview to provide beforehand an indication of topics to be covered and, possibly, some of the questions to be asked. The ostensible reason is that statistics, etc., can be provided at the meeting. Really though, says Gooding, it's because one of the first rules in business is that 'there should be no surprises'.

Importantly, this forces the journalist to research and think carefully about how the interview should be structured. Thorough research for business interviews is essential, Gooding says.

> 'The journalist needs to have a clear idea of what he/she wants to achieve or the interviewee will set the agenda and take complete control. Read the cuttings, talk to competitors, prepare soft questions, not-so-soft questions and the approach you will use when asking the hard questions.'

No need to waste time on preliminaries – a quick greeting and get down to business. You definitely need to know how long you have, as business interviews very rarely overrun.

Beware, Gooding says, of the PR who wishes to sit behind you (see p. 147). Be aware that any attempts to flatter you are designed to make you feel better disposed to the company and to take up your valuable time in an unproductive way. 'Why otherwise would a captain of industry ask a journalist who probably has never run a whelk stall, for an opinion on how the company should operate?'

Few executives will talk freely to a journalist they neither know nor trust. One way to gain trust is to be flexible. Gooding suggests:

> 'Offer to go off the record at any time the interviewee wishes to. And, to emphasise your trustworthiness, ostentatiously switch off your tape recorder. You might even allow some second thoughts and when an executive says "I think that should be off the record" go along with it. You can learn more and have a better understanding of the company's business that way.'

Obviously, he says, executives very rarely go on the record when dishing the dirt on competitors. 'Often, if a journalist is to fully understand a complex situation, some confidential background has to be provided by an off-the-record briefing.'

It's comforting, he concludes, that although during the interview the corporation holds most of the cards, the journalist is in charge of the material. However, he believes specialists need to tread a careful line.

'You're not going to be very effective if you upset too many people in the industry so they talk to you only under sufferance. On the other hand, you don't want to be seen as an industry "mouthpiece" and part of its PR efforts.

Only by doing the research, knowing as much as possible about the full picture, by being accurate and fair in your reporting and comments, can you achieve this. When you say you won't quote someone, you don't quote him. When you give undertakings, you stick to them.'

VULNERABLE PEOPLE

At some time during their careers, many journalists have to interview vulnerable people: perhaps distraught middle-aged parents whose only daughter is in a coma after a hit-and-run accident, or a confused and frightened 70-year-old man whose hip has been broken in a mugging, or a young mother whose child has been abducted.

These interviews are often easier than the beginner expects. Provided you are sympathetic and take your time and listen, the story will usually pour out. What stops the flow is brisk or brusque efficiency in getting to the facts. This clearly shows a lack of empathy, coupled with a 'hurry-up-for-pity's-sake-I'm-on-deadline' approach, reducing the interviewee to info fodder.

The bereaved and injured are in shock, so talking about what's happened usually helps them, acting as some form of therapy. The emotionally vulnerable, by contrast, are usually wary and very reluctant to relive painful events or talk about unusual behaviour that is condemned or not understood by the majority. Interviewing them is much harder and requires delicacy.

It is a great help to be introduced to them by someone they have faith in – their counsellor, therapist or social worker – and it's essential before you meet them to put yourself, as much as possible, into their shoes. How would you feel if at 82, your beloved wife of 60 years developed Alzheimer's and you were too frail to cope with 24-hour care? How would you feel if you discovered your son was abusing other children at his school? How would you react if your husband left you for another man?

Gaining trust

Slowly and very gently is the way to approach vulnerable people. You have to gain their trust if they're to tell you their story. This takes time. Freelance Joy Melville, who has specialised in such interviews, says you must never rush. 'You cannot just march in.'

When interviewing British orphans who had been shipped off to Australia, Canada and New Zealand in the 1930s, many of whom had been horrifically abused by foster families, she found on the first or second visit that, even though they had agreed to speak to her, these people became very upset and burst into tears. 'Often it was only on the third visit that I felt able to say "Would you mind if I took some notes?"'

It's crucial, she says, to accept any offer of tea these people make. She instances just one exception which occurred when she interviewed a woman who was obsessive about dirt and germs.

> 'I had permission from her therapist to see her and when I got there she had put sheets all the way down the hall, right through the sitting room and all over the chair where I was going to sit. The therapist had warned me whatever I did, not to go to the loo because it would have taken her a day to ensure it was properly clean.
>
> But I said yes to tea, thinking it would put her at her ease. She watched me intently while I drank the tea and when I finished she leapt up and I think she spent 25 minutes in the kitchen scouring the cup and saucer.'

Vulnerable interviewees are particularly suspicious and need to be convinced that you understand and approve of what they're revealing about themselves. 'They're picking up signs all the time,' Melville says. 'I often say, "Oh yes, I do agree, because the same has happened to me." If they feel you aren't shocked, they're encouraged to say "And there's another thing . . ."'

It often helps, she says, to put yourself down deliberately, for instance by saying 'Oh yes, every single man I've ever known has dropped me.' This may or may not be true, she says, but you're trying not to upstage them. 'You're saying they're not the only person who's experienced this, the only person who's mucked it up. They mustn't think that everyone else copes better than they do.'

Always be sympathetic

Encapsulated advice for interviewers is usually: 'Be sceptical, not adversarial'. Encapsulated advice when interviewing the emotionally vulnerable is: 'Never be anything other than sympathetic'.

Melville instances agoraphobics, men and women who have a fear of leaving, or going any distance from, home.

> 'Agoraphobics never starve. There's always a husband, a neighbour, who does the shopping. If the husband dies or the neighbour moves away, the agoraphobic will venture out a short distance to find someone else – but if you even imply they could go outside, they say, "You don't understand, do you? You just don't understand how I feel. Have you ever had a phobia yourself?" And they work themselves up into an absolute anger and then they can say: "It's useless. Why don't you go?"'

Instead of challenging an agoraphobic, you get results by being sympathetic and interested, Melville says, by asking oblique questions. 'How do the children get to school? Who takes them?' Your face, she says, often becomes 'a mask of sympathy'.

No laughing matter

Just as important as never passing negative judgments on what a vulnerable person tells you is never laughing. Melville remembers a woman who was arachnophobic: terrified of spiders.

> 'She told me, "I saw this spider and I threw a telephone directory at it and it moved four inches to the left and defied me!" It was very hard not to say, "Did it have a gun?" as opposed to "How awful", but I don't like spiders so I was sympathetic. It's often very hard not to laugh but you must never, ever.
>
> You put your hand over your mouth and pull the skin of your cheekbones back, all the time looking down at your notebook, then no one can see your eyes laughing.'

Or else you can turn an incipient laugh into a cough or, as a last resort, bite the inside of your cheeks – then it's impossible to laugh.

Melville uses shorthand and believes that the fact she is not staring intently at people but looking down at her notebook and then glancing up to smile at appropriate moments often encourages confidences. 'A chiropodist once told me he heard the most amazing things from people *because* he had his back to them, working on their feet.' This is not accepted wisdom in journalism, which sets great store by eye contact, but consider: the same principle is employed by the priest in the confessional or by the psychiatrist, sitting out of sight of the patient on the couch.

Interviewing the seriously mentally ill can be traumatic for the interviewer. Melville once went to interview a schizophrenic young woman of about 18.

> 'Her mother opened the door, looking very old and tired with the trauma she was going through with her daughter. The daughter was in a nest of blankets and she leapt up, looked at me and said "Right after you phoned I decided to shave my head," and she had.
>
> This was a very difficult interview because at the same time she was talking to me she was also having a conversation with King Tutankhamun. She'd say something to me and then look over her shoulder and say "I don't see why I should die young just because you died young. Just because you died young, doesn't mean I've got to" and then she'd go on talking to me.
>
> At one point, she suddenly scribbled something down on a piece of paper, scrunched it up, threw it down and ran out of the room. Of course in true journalistic style I leapt for the wastepaper basket. She'd written "I know where I'm going but I don't want to go."

It was really very, very sad. Afterwards I felt I had to go and talk to her mother and say thank you, because the mother never got out of the house, had this daughter rampaging round, sometimes running out of the house at 2 o'clock in the morning.'

The long goodbye

Just as it takes longer to start the interview, testing the emotional temperature, so it takes much longer to say goodbye. The interview may be over but you shouldn't leave until you're sure your interviewee is contented. Melville says:

'People who have been living on tranquillisers, for instance, are extremely vulnerable. After you've talked to them for a while you may know you have got enough for the article, but it's at that point they have decided you are sympathetic and understanding.

If you leave that house within four hours you are very lucky. They absolutely offload everything on to you. In effect you are the stranger on the train to whom they can tell all, not the relation who said "I told you not to marry him!" or the neighbour who said "Oh dear, does he really do that?"

You may be exhausted but you have turned into the therapist. You feel they have allowed you into their home and that you can't just walk into their lives, interview them, say "Thank you very much" and walk out again. The dailies do and sometimes afterwards, they won't talk to journalists again.'

CHILDREN

For wonderful and unexpected quotes go to a child, but go carefully, because interviewing children is more difficult than it looks and is hedged with complications. The Press Complaints Commission's directions are clear.

Young people should be free to complete their time at school without unnecessary intrusion. Journalists should not interview or photograph children under the age of 16 on subjects involving the welfare of the child or of any other child in the absence of or without the consent of a parent or other adult who is responsible for the children.

There's also a whole section offering guidance on interviewing/reporting children involved in sex cases.

The hazardous ages in interviewing children are from 4 to 10. During that time children have a tendency to say yes, being unwilling to contradict an adult who's interviewing them. With teenagers, of course, the opposite can be true. They may delight in defying, shocking or confusing adults.

Questions to younger children shouldn't suggest an answer. Not: 'Did you enjoy that film?' Rather: 'What did you think of that film?' And of course younger children shouldn't be helped with an answer. If they're feeling shy, embarrassed or if they don't understand what you're talking about, they may well answer by saying they don't know. You also must accept they may become tongue-tied because transfixed by your ears, your spectacles or something else going on in the room. Try to keep interviews with youngsters short and avoid noisy places full of distractions and interruptions.

Sarah McCrum and Lotte Hughes of Save the Children have written a booklet, *Interviewing Children* (1998), full of valuable advice, most of it pure common sense: listen, don't interrupt, see children as individuals with thoughts and feelings deserving attention, choose where to interview carefully.

Take care with words

Choose your words with care. Even younger teenagers will bridle if asked if they'd 'give a child's perspective on . . .' Call them young people. Young prostitutes may prefer the description 'hostess' or 'sex worker'.

In summary, the booklet sets out what children want interviewers to do:

- let them to speak for themselves without adult interference
- treat them as equals
- see them as individuals with their own thoughts, enthusiasm and concerns
- let them speak freely
- value their experiences
- take their opinions seriously.

Interviewing Children covers where to find children to interview, thoughts on selection and obtaining permission.

> The wishes and rights of children need to be balanced against those of parents or guardians. But we think that children's wishes and best interests should be paramount – because they have the right to speak out, and adults don't have the right to silence them.
>
> This becomes a thorny issue when you want to talk to minors who are, say, in local government care. (They might be living on the street, but still officially in 'care'.) Or they could be young offenders in an institution, or under-age soldiers in an army – all situations where adults in authority may say you can't interview the children because they are at risk, or somehow spoken for.

Ask the children

In the UK, the law says that you must get permission from the local authority to interview young people under 18 who are in care. But the booklet suggests you ask the children what they want.

> Leave it to the child to decide whether or not they want to be quoted ... Adults (particularly officials) may try to gag children because they are afraid of what they might say, or afraid it will show them in a bad light. But their classic excuse for trying to stop children being interviewed is that the children are vulnerable and need to be protected. That's rather patronising. The same thing used to be said about women.

When an interview has been set up with children, the booklet advises an exploratory visit to prepare the ground, allowing plenty of time for the interview, sitting at the children's level and answering the children's curiosity about yourself and any tape recorders or shorthand you might be using. There is also advice on drawing out the reluctant, interviewing abroad when using a translator, and ways to end the interview.

DEATH KNOCKS

Tragedy makes good copy. The best interviewers appreciate this and, at the same time, sympathise with the people they interview, a fact that comes through clearly again and again from talking to journalists experienced in 'death knocks' or 'fatals'. Former Birmingham *Evening Mail* journalist Sue White says:

> 'In some ways, doing a fatal is almost as easy as court reporting. You've got to listen, that's the key. You're given the general facts and you get them confirmed. You can sit in with people and they will tell you everything. To be frank, I rather enjoyed interviewing people whose relatives had died in car crashes or traumatic circumstances.'

Reporters most often get details of deaths from routine calls to the police, ambulance and fire services. The desk officer provides the basic information: name, address (if these are available) and how the body was found and where. Depending on the time and whether it's a morning, evening or weekly paper, the reporter may write up the story so far for the next edition or go straight out to the house/scene of death. As White recounts:

> 'If the death had happened overnight, say a 17-year-old boy on a motorbike, I'd write the story for the first edition and then set off, not knowing what I would find. Normally it would be quiet and I'd knock on the door. It would open a crack and someone would answer.
>   I'd know from the police if the boy lived at home, so – it's an intuitive thing – I'd say "Hello, I'm Sue White from the Birmingham *Evening*

Mail. We've heard from the police about the dreadful accident last night. Could I come in and have a word with you about it?" Almost everyone would say "All right".'

Death today is sanitised, tidied away and few people under 30 have seen a dead body or experienced bereavement. They may not realise that after a death, relatives are in shock and often have a need to talk freely.

Checking details

'If it was a neighbour who answered, they might not know what to do and would bring the mother or father to the door. It's important to be very, very courteous and understanding. I'd repeat where I was from and that we wanted to check we had all the details correct.

I'd be taken in and sat in the lounge. It would be very quiet, they'd be stunned. I felt if I talked openly, in as friendly and sympathetic a way as possible – one person to another, making it clear I just wanted to confirm some facts – people would give me that information. I was usually right.

What they tell you leads on to further questions. They'd say, "And he was just about to get married," and you'd think the story is getting better. "Oh, really," I'd say. They'd tell me about her and I'd ask, "Would you mind if we went and had a word?" Normally there would be no objection, provided I had appeared sympathetic and understanding.

I always made out I was double-checking, because that way they feel they are not being grilled. It's a sympathetic way of leading them into answering questions and their responses will reveal more of the story. I never felt I was taking advantage of anybody. They want to unburden themselves. It all just flows out.

After I'd established what had happened and that I genuinely wanted to hear about it, the rest of the story would come out. How long he'd had the bike, that he was a leading light in the club and had won trophies or that he'd had a row with his girlfriend and was on his way to say sorry . . . a tremendous story, I'd think.

If it was a young girl killed in a car crash, I'd ask what sort of car she was driving and they'd say "Well, it was a Ford Fiesta and she did love it." "Why?" I'd ask. "Because her father scrimped and saved and put all his money from when he was made redundant by Rover into buying her that car . . ." And there's your story, particularly if there'd been trouble at Rover.'

Think pix

After a while and they'd gone quiet, I'd say, "By the way, have you any photographs of him, a nice picture we could put in the paper?" They'd rummage about in the sideboard and bring out a choice of pictures. I'd know which was the one the paper would use, but I'd take them all, to make sure the *Express and Star* [opposition] didn't get them. They'd do the same to us.'

Always promise you'll take good care of the pix and plan to return them personally – and mean it. Your paper's reputation is involved. Ensure the photos are identified with name and address written in a *soft 2B pencil* on the back, not with a ball-point pen, and do make it plain when passing any photographs on to layout, picture desk or production how important it is that they must be returned.

If journalists from competing papers arrive on the doorstep at the same time, they'll do a joint interview and share the pix, perhaps phoning back separately for additional quotes. If the opposition gets there first and takes all the pictures offered, the relatives will be able to find some more from somewhere but they may not be as good.

Suspicious circumstances

'If the fatal was something good like a murder, I'd go straight out to the address I'd been given by the police or the ambulance men,' says White. 'If it wasn't clear how the child or person died and no one had been charged, you're free to report it. So I'd knock on the door.'

Relatives of someone who has died in suspicious circumstances are just as shocked as relatives of someone who has died in an accident but there are certainly added emotions, ranging from anger or shame to blame and guilt. So the doorstep reaction is less certain.

> 'Some slam the door in your face but it didn't happen very often to me. With one story we had to track down the relatives of three members of a family found gassed in a car in their garage. A colleague went to see one set of grandparents and I went to the other. I had a feeling it was not going to be good.
> She didn't slam the door but started shouting at me on the doorstep, then chased me down the front garden path yelling "Sod off!" I think the *Express and Star* had got to her before we did. So I went to the neighbours.'

If the relative is incensed it's wise to start with neighbours on the same side of the road but not visible from the relative's house. It's rare that neighbours can't give you something.

If a relative who has refused an interview then sees the reporter talking to a neighbour, they may try to prevent the interview.

> 'One man who wouldn't talk bawled at me, so – because you don't come away without a story – I went across the road, but a few doors away, so he couldn't see me. He stormed after me into this bloke's garden, shouting "You can't do this – I'm going to call the police." It's very important to be polite. If you retaliate you lose it. So I said "Yes, actually I can," and I went on interviewing.'

Once the initial shock has passed, the reaction of most people to a relative's preventable death is to wish for recognition of the dead person's life and to hope that their death has not been in vain. A sympathetic interview and accurate report can meet both these wishes and often brings an added journalistic reward, as in this story from Sue White.

> 'A 24-year-old woman with two young children had to have a heart transplant. Her husband had died the year before from a brain haemorrhage. She was a really nice, quiet, gentle woman and I interviewed her at her mother's house before the operation.
>
> After she'd had the new heart I checked back every day with relatives and the hospital. The operation had been fine but a week later she caught an infection and died. Her husband had been buried in his wedding suit and, talking to the grandmother, it came out that the 24-year-old was to be buried in her wedding dress. Superb.'

You may wince at that last word, but you must recognise that the journalist would not have been welcomed into the house three times if she hadn't been a sympathetic, understanding reporter and that what she wrote was accurate and had passed intense scrutiny. It's fairly certain that the stories comforted the grieving relatives who still treasure the cuttings.

Part of the job

However much you may hate this type of interviewing, it's part of a journalist's job. A regional newspaper reporter asked to contact a famous former football manager whose son had committed suicide, refused. He said it would damage the close personal relationship he had with the manager, and he was not prepared to accept an alternative job, which he considered a demotion.

An employment tribunal decided against him, judging that the editor and the paper had acted reasonably throughout. 'Although the circumstances were tragic for [the former manager] this was a matter of national importance and it was an opportunity for a local paper to obtain a scoop.' The reporter lost his claim for unfair dismissal.

Self-interest dictates that local paper journalists dealing with a local tragedy proceed circumspectly. It's a different matter with the national press covering a national disaster. Fiercely competitive reporters descend and do what's necessary to get the story and accompanying pix. They know they're unlikely to return to the same street in the next five years and it's a licence to behave badly – and some do.

A trainee on a tabloid Sunday was told, 'There's been a murder. Go and get an interview and we'll send a photographer.' The two of them talked their way in, got the interview and the photographs. The photographer then became incredibly aggressive, so much so that the woman threw them both out. Afterwards, the trainee asked 'Why did you do that?' 'Well,' said the photographer, 'the next paper that comes along won't get in.'

'When Fleet Street goes home, we're still here'

After the 1999 Paddington rail disaster, the full media circus descended on Reading where most of the dead had lived – TV, radio, broadsheet and tabloid reporters. Some journalists besieged bereaved relatives' houses, with the result that neighbours attacked them. On one occasion, the police were called.

To avoid extra harassment of grieving relatives, rival Reading local paper editors decided not to do any death knocks but to let relatives approach them if they wished. One commented:

> 'We're putting our usual rivalries aside on this. The national press is all over Reading like a rash and it's going to be bad enough for relatives coping with that. We're mindful of the fact that when Fleet Street goes back home, we're still here.'

Editors of papers in towns where fewer had died disagreed. 'I don't see why if someone dies in a train crash, they should not have an obituary in the paper,' said one. 'Obituaries are not just dabbling in death for the sake of it. They are there to record someone's life.'

PRS AND TWO-HANDERS

The truism couldn't be truer: two's company, three's a crowd. PRs sitting in on interviews can be a real drag. Playing gooseberry, they sour that special one-to-one relationship that's at the heart of a good interview. Probably the best way to take it is as a compliment. You're so good that a watchdog is needed.

One on two

Royals, government ministers and certain chief executives of multinationals always have a PR present as well as a tape recorder running. With a smaller organisation, when a PR sits in, it's probably because the interviewee is inexperienced or very nervous.

Alan Russell, who has worked in PR on both sides of the Atlantic, says some clients are so intimidated by journalists that they ask PRs to sit in for protection. 'But,' he says, 'the PR has to sit there absolutely stumm. It's very tempting to offer answers when you feel your client is not doing very well, but you have to fight against it.'

With the exception of royal and government press officers, PRs who wish to sit in and are doing their job properly will ask if you mind their being present. Unless it was a condition of the interview, you are entitled to reply 'Yes' but it's probably wisest not to. The essential thing is to ensure they are sitting in full view. If they say modestly 'I'll just tuck myself away here' (behind you), beware. This means they can signal to the interviewee when danger threatens, when to change tack, when to produce a red herring.

You must ensure you can see both of them. Ideally, fix it so that they are facing you and eye contact between them is restricted. Some journalists when offered a chair accept it and stay where they are put. Not always wise. All you have to say is 'Do you mind? I'd be much happier over here.' There's no need to give a reason. Or you can make a joke of it saying 'I want to keep my eyes on both of you!' These are all accepted manoeuvres in a constantly played game.

The positive side of having a PR present is that they can be useful, adding points of detail that the interviewee doesn't have to hand or saving a lot of time by agreeing to provide missing information later. They may leave the room to fetch necessary paperwork. That's your opportunity. If you're really lucky, the PR will be called away to the phone during the interview. Now that's worth thinking about.

Journalists depend on PRs more than most of us will admit, which makes the PR love–hate relationship with journalists easy to understand. Because PRs understand the way journalists think, they are able to feed journalists with ideas, copy and pictures specifically tailored for individual readerships. On the journalist's part this makes for dependence.

Because they understand the way journalists think, PRs are able to advise their clients how to resist interviewers' wiles. 'Never do an interview at home,' they counsel. 'Gives away too much about you. Try an anonymous hotel room instead . . . It's important to come prepared for questions on . . . Beware the tricky question, based on rumours . . .' On the journalist's part this makes for intense irritation.

Interviewing PRs

When interviewing PRs, be straightforward and direct. They understand journalists far too well to be fooled by attempts at guile. They've sat in on too many interviews where the journalists have missed the real story to be impressed. Most importantly, they have good memories. Not selective, like journalists, but based on letters and tearsheets: what we said and what we delivered.

Two on one

There may come occasions when you find yourself doing a two-handed interview: two journalists, one interviewee. This may be because time is limited and the interviewee decides to talk to feature writers from a weekly and a monthly publication at the same time. Since you're not immediate competitors, this is possible though not desirable.

You may be a specialist interviewing someone so prestigious that your editor (not a specialist in your area) wants to join you. Or you may be one of two specialists from the same paper coming at the interviewee from different angles. In each instance it's important to work out together beforehand how the questioning will be shared and who will start. Maybe equally – for example, 'I'll ask the first question, you ask the second.' Then you have to agree how many follow-up questions are admissible. This can be tricky for the interviewee, since the questioning may swing wildly from subject to subject, so give them fair warning. The alternative is to agree to interview, say, 10 minutes at a time.

Problems arise if one interviewer from a competing publication breaks the agreement to share interviewing time equally and hogs the questioning. If you're by nature kind, considerate and polite, then ask to be sent on an assertiveness course. You're there to get a story, not to let the other reporter get their story.

Three, four and five-handers are definitely to be avoided. One hapless feature writer from a teenage magazine found at the last minute that her one-on-one interview with Tom Cruise turned into a four-hander: herself and three middle-aged Dutchmen. The film involved flying stunts and despite the poor woman's best efforts, the conversation turned technical and she was frozen out while the men discussed F-14s. Putting yourself in her position, it's tough. Put yourself in Tom Cruise's position, and it's a great relief. She'd wanted to ask him whether he preferred Y-fronts or boxer shorts.

Ah, journalism.

12

Law and ethics

Wynford Hicks

If you want to be a competent professional interviewer, talent, skill and experience are essential – but they are not enough. You must also know and understand the law as it applies to journalists and be familiar with the professional and ethical issues of journalism, particularly as defined in the Press Complaints Commission's code of practice.

The PCC code and a similar one issued by the National Union of Journalists are included in this chapter, but there is no such concise and convenient summary of the law as it applies to journalists. Even a complete chapter on it would be inadequate: you need a good textbook, such as *McNae's Essential Law for Journalists* (Greenwood and Welsh, 1999).

LAW FOR JOURNALISTS

Make sure you get hold of the latest edition of this textbook since media law changes constantly. Indeed the Human Rights Act, which came into force last year (October 2000), is certain to have a big influence in two key areas: privacy on the one hand, and on the other, libel and other constraints on publication.

The Act incorporates into UK law the European Convention on Human Rights, which includes the following clauses:

Right to respect for private and family life
1. Everyone has the right to respect for his private and family life, his home and his correspondence.

Freedom of expression
1. Everyone has the right to freedom of expression. This right shall include freedom to hold opinions and to receive and impart information and ideas without interference by public authority and regardless of frontiers . . .

Essentially these new rights will strengthen both the case for privacy against intrusion by journalists – and the case for vigorous public discussion even if individuals are criticised. Although these new rights will be influential, it is impossible to predict exactly how judges in the UK will interpret and apply them. As a libel specialist wrote in *The Times* (3 October 2000): 'Only by watching the drama as it unfolds in future cases in the Royal Courts of Justice will we see whether and how the balance between freedom of expression and privacy is likely to change in the UK.'

Libel

Libel is the most powerful constraint on journalists. Possibly because it is so tough its scope is exaggerated by some people including journalists – even some of those who train and advise them. For example, two books on interviewing (*Interviewing for Journalists* by Joan Clayton and *Interviewing Techniques for Writers & Researchers* by Susan Dunne) make the misleading claim that true and accurate statements can be libellous.

Justification

In fact, as McNae points out: 'It is a complete defence to a libel action . . . to prove that the words complained of are true.' This defence is known as 'justification'.

The 'Venetian blind'

The confusion probably comes from the notorious difficulty journalists face in proving the truth of the words complained of – as is shown by a string of cases where libel juries have got it wrong. For example, writing in the *Guardian* (18 March 2000), Geoffrey Wheatcroft recalled what Labour Party wits called the 'Venetian blind':

> 'In 1957, an article in the *Spectator* skittishly suggested that three Labour politicians had been drinking a good deal at a socialist conference in Venice. The three, Aneurin Bevan, Richard Crossman and Morgan Phillips, sued, testified on oath to their sobriety, and won large damages.
> Fifteen years later, Crossman boasted (in my presence) that they had indeed all been toping heavily, and that at least one of them had been blind drunk.'

The fact is that in libel cases where justification is claimed, it is for the defendant to prove the truth of the words complained of – there is no presumption of innocence, as in other legal proceedings.

Other defences

There are other defences to libel. The main ones are:

- fair comment (not 'fair' in the sense of 'just' but comment based on an honestly held opinion)
- privilege (statements made for example in court or at a public meeting)
- accord and satisfaction (e.g. the publication of a correction and apology, accepted by the plaintiff).

Others include:

- that the plaintiff has died – the dead are not protected by the law of libel, which explains why the death of Robert Maxwell was followed by a tidal wave of hostile comment (while he was alive he intimidated the press by constantly issuing libel writs)
- that the plaintiff agreed to the publication – a signed statement from them, if you could obtain one, would obviously do the trick.

Two other points weigh heavily against the defendant. First, it is not necessary for the plaintiff to prove that the defendant *intended* to libel them. For example, by printing an interviewee's libellous comment on a third party – without in any way endorsing it – you publish the libel.

Also, the test of whether a statement is defamatory has nothing to do with the meaning intended by the person who made it or published it. Instead it's the meaning that 'a reasonable person' would understand it to have. Innuendo – a hidden meaning – is dangerous. For example, 'tired and emotional', the *Private Eye* euphemism for drunk, might well be considered to have this meaning even if the journalist using the phrase meant it literally.

Second, it is not necessary to prove that the words complained of have actually damaged the reputation of the plaintiff – merely that they *tended* to do so.

A statement can be defamatory of a person if it tends to do any one of the following:

- expose them to hatred, ridicule or contempt
- cause them to be shunned or avoided
- lower them in the estimation of right-thinking members of society generally
- disparage them in their business, trade, office or profession.

So, faced with this legal minefield, what is the journalist to do? A very common cause of libel actions is the failure to apply professional standards of accuracy and fairness. Most libel actions can be avoided.

Make and keep accurate notes

Some of the cases cited in McNae are hair-raising. For example, when in 1997 the *Sunday Times* was trying to prove the truth of a story about Albert Reynolds, the former Irish prime minister, the reporter who wrote the story told the court he had no notes. 'I was not in note-taking mode,' he said.

Having made accurate notes, keep them and any tapes for one year after your story is published. The Defamation Act 1996 reduced the time within which an action must be started to one year after publication.

Check the cuttings – and what you're told in the interview

Remember that cuttings are only a starting point: they should never be assumed to be accurate, so check the content with the interviewee.

If a cutting contains a libellous statement and you republish it, this is called a fresh publication – and creates a fresh cause of action. The plaintiff can now sue you for libel whether or not they sued the original publisher.

Then, if your interviewee says something defamatory about another person, can it be proved to be true? Will your interviewee stand by their statement and can they back it up to the satisfaction of a jury?

Legal advice

Libel experts make various suggestions about how you can reduce the chance of being sued or at least improve your chances of winning in court. One is to persuade your interviewee to make a signed statement confirming what they say; if they die or change their minds, you have something to back up your story.

Another is to have your copy – or the factual parts of it – checked by the person or organisation concerned. This idea runs counter to journalistic tradition (and in some confrontational stories is clearly impractical) but it is worth considering.

Finally, if you think your story is potentially libellous, you (or your editor) should take legal advice. On some publications page proofs are routinely legalled (checked by a lawyer) before publication.

Slander

Whereas libel is defamation in permanent or broadcast form, slander is usually spoken. In theory a journalist can slander somebody merely by asking questions – but this is rare.

Malicious falsehood

This is publication of a false statement likely to damage somebody. By contrast with libel, the plaintiff must prove that the statement is untrue and that it is made maliciously.

Copyright

Copyright particularly concerns interviewers in two ways: first, when you use cuttings, you must not lift large chunks verbatim from the original story. As well as being bad practice professionally – the material is unchecked, your readers (who may have seen the original) are being short-changed – this is a breach of copyright.

There is now copyright in the spoken word as soon as it is recorded (with or without the speaker's permission) and it belongs to the speaker. When somebody agrees to be interviewed, they are assumed to agree that their words can be recorded and published. But if they do not give their consent, there may be a breach of copyright.

Trespass, harassment, breach of confidence

Although there is no law of privacy (but see the opening section of this chapter), legal action to protect it is possible under other headings, such as trespass, harassment and breach of confidence.

The traditional warning 'Trespassers will be prosecuted' is something of an empty threat. First, trespass is defined as injuring land, goods or the person: merely walking on to a person's property is unlikely to do much damage. Second, it is a civil rather than a criminal matter: the owner sues for damages. But the owner is entitled to ask trespassers to leave private property – and to use reasonable force to eject them – so if you're asked to leave, you must do so.

Many apparently 'public' places are in fact private property. For example, a shopping centre and the forecourt of a bus station are obvious places to conduct vox pop interviews – journalists should not be intimidated from entering them. But security guards acting for the owner are legally entitled to ask you to leave.

Harassment is now recognised as an offence under the Protection from Harassment Act 1997. Although harassment is not defined in the Act, it is defined in the PCC code (see below).

The law of confidentiality bans the publication of material that has been gathered in confidence, as when a domestic servant reveals private information about their employer. This was the law used in 1989 in the case of Bill Goodwin, a trainee reporter working for *Engineer* magazine.

Goodwin received information from a source inside an engineering company and phoned them to check it. The company's response was to obtain an injunction restraining the *Engineer* from publishing the story and an order requiring Goodwin to hand over notes that would reveal his source. When he refused, he was fined £5,000 – though in 1996 the European Court of Human Rights decided that the order and the fine violated his right to freedom of expression.

CODES OF CONDUCT/PRACTICE

The two most important codes for print journalists are those of the National Union of Journalists and the Press Complaints Commission. There are also several codes for broadcast journalists; the Chartered Institute of Journalists has its own code; and there is a set of guidelines for covering sex issues if you work on a teenage magazine.

The NUJ code of conduct

The NUJ has had a code of conduct for its members since the late 1930s. For a time, during the 1980s, attempts were made to enforce the code by considering complaints against individual journalists. But this practice was not widely supported and has been abandoned. Now the code is seen by the NUJ as a target for journalists to aim for rather than a means to punish those who fail to abide by it. But the objection remains: surely a code of conduct is weakened if there is no way of enforcing it and no sanction against those who flout it.

The NUJ code has traditionally consisted of general statements of high principle but recent amendments (e.g. to clause 10; the new clause 11) are inclined to go into more detail. In clause 10 political correctness has now added 'age' to the list of unmentionables and 'ridicule' to the list of what not to encourage. Will some cumbersome and pompous phrase defining 'physical characteristics' be next? David Yelland, editor of the *Sun*, once wrote to that bastion of political correctness the *Guardian* wittily objecting to a diary reference to his baldness. In this climate what happens to political cartoons – or jokes in general?

By contrast, the phrase 'overriding considerations of the public interest' used in two key clauses (5 and 6, covering subterfuge and intrusion) is nowhere defined.

The wording of clause 5 (on subterfuge) betrays muddled thinking – or unresolved disagreement. The first sentence unequivocally bans subterfuge. The second says it is justified only in the public interest. The third says that a journalist is entitled to object to subterfuge – as an individual. On this point the PCC code clause 11 on misrepresentation makes better sense: it is clearer and more coherent.

Curiously, the code nowhere mentions 'quotes' or even 'interviews' so there is no specific guidance on obtaining or editing quotes. But references to 'obtaining information' can be assumed to apply to interviewing.

Clause 12 surely goes too far. It would ban a wine writer on assignment from buying a case of wine before their piece recommending it was published. Compare the clause with the PCC's clause 14, which is sensibly restricted to financial journalism.

Most of the general instructions that follow are admirable and should be followed – but they are better expressed in the PCC code. Phrases like 'afford the right of reply to persons criticised' betray the NUJ code's ancient origins.

---

1   A journalist has a duty to maintain the highest professional and ethical standards.

2   A journalist shall at all times defend the principle of the freedom of the press and other media in relation to the collection of information and the expression of comment and criticism. He/she shall strive to eliminate distortion, news suppression and censorship.

3   A journalist shall strive to ensure that the information he/she disseminates is fair and accurate, avoid the expression of comment and conjecture as established fact and falsification by distortion, selection or misrepresentation.

4   A journalist shall rectify promptly any harmful inaccuracies, ensure that correction and apologies receive due prominence and afford the right of reply to persons criticised when the issue is of sufficient importance.

5   A journalist shall obtain information, photographs and illustrations only by straightforward means. The use of other means can be justified only by overriding considerations of the public interest. The journalist is entitled to exercise a personal conscientious objection to the use of such means.

6   A journalist shall do nothing which entails intrusion into anybody's private life, grief or distress, subject to justification by overriding considerations of the public interest.

7   A journalist shall protect confidential sources of information.

8   A journalist shall not accept bribes nor shall he/she allow other inducements to influence the performance of his/her professional duties.

9   A journalist shall not lend himself/herself to the distortion or suppression of the truth because of advertising or other considerations.

10   A journalist shall mention a person's age, sex, race, colour, creed, illegitimacy, disability, marital status, or sexual orientation only if this information is strictly relevant. A journalist shall neither originate nor process material which encourages discrimination, ridicule, prejudice or hatred on any of the above-mentioned grounds.

11   No journalist shall knowingly cause or allow the publication or broadcast of a photograph that has been manipulated unless that photograph is clearly labelled as such. Manipulated does not include normal dodging, burning, colour balancing, spotting, contrast adjustment, cropping and obvious masking for legal or safety reasons.

12   A journalist shall not take private advantage of information gained in the course of his/her duties before the information is public knowledge.

13   A journalist shall not by way of statement, voice or appearance endorse by advertisement any commercial product or service save for the promotion of his/her own work or of the medium by which he/she is employed.

The PCC code of practice

The Press Complaints Commission was set up by the industry in 1991 in response to the Calcutt committee's tough warning that if the press did not clean up its act it would face statutory regulation. The code of practice drafted by a committee of editors was based on an existing code of the Newspaper Publishers Association and proposals from the Calcutt committee and the former Press Council. It has since been amended in response to various events, such as the furore over alleged press harassment of Princess Diana. (The version below dates from 1 December 1999.)

Note clause 3 on privacy ('Everyone is entitled to respect for his or her private and family life, home, health and correspondence.') which is similar to a key clause in the European Convention on Human Rights.

The PCC code goes into far more detail than the NUJ code, particularly in defining 'the public interest', which can apply to a number of clauses. Although in general the PCC code reads better than the NUJ code, it has occasional lapses. In places it adopts a similar sub-legal language: pursuing journalists are 'asked to desist', for example. And why the reference in clause 4 to 'journalists *and* photographers' – aren't photographers journalists?

More seriously, the code sometimes refers to 'newspapers and periodicals', 'the press' and sometimes to 'newspapers'. This tends to obscure the fact that in all respects the code applies to periodicals as well as newspapers.

Occasionally, a qualifying adjective raises rather than answers a question: in clause 6 young people are to be protected from '*unnecessary* intrusion' – what would '*necessary* intrusion' be?

Once again 'quotes' are not mentioned and the word 'interview' is used only once (in clause 6 on children). But there are references to 'making enquiries', to 'telephoning, questioning, pursuing' people and to 'stories' as well as to obtaining information. Taken as a whole the code gives journalists useful and relevant guidance on a number of controversial points.

---

1   Accuracy
(i)   Newspapers and periodicals must take care not to publish inaccurate, misleading or distorted material including pictures.
(ii) Whenever it is recognised that a significant inaccuracy, misleading statement or distorted report has been published, it must be corrected promptly and with due prominence.

(iii) An apology must be published whenever appropriate.

(iv) Newspapers, whilst free to be partisan, must distinguish clearly between comment, conjecture and fact.

(v) A newspaper or periodical must report fairly and accurately the outcome of an action for defamation to which it has been a party.

2   Opportunity to reply
       A fair opportunity to reply to inaccuracies must be given to individuals or organisations when reasonably called for.

3   Privacy*
(i)   Everyone is entitled to respect for his or her private and family life, home, health and correspondence. A publication will be expected to justify intrusions into any individual's private life without consent.

(ii)   The use of long lens photography to take pictures of people in private places without their consent is unacceptable.
       Note: private places are public or private property where there is a reasonable expectation of privacy.

4   Harassment*
(i)   Journalists and photographers must neither obtain nor seek to obtain information or pictures through intimidation, harassment or persistent pursuit.

(ii)   They must not photograph individuals in private places (as defined in the note to clause 3) without their consent; must not persist in telephoning, questioning, pursuing or photographing individuals after having been asked to desist; must not remain on their property after having been asked to leave and must not follow them.

(iii) Editors must ensure that those working for them comply with these requirements and must not publish material from other sources which does not meet these requirements.

5   Intrusion into grief or shock
       In cases involving grief or shock, enquiries must be carried out and approaches made with sympathy and discretion. Publication must be handled sensitively at such times, but this should not be interpreted as restricting the right to report judicial proceedings.

6   Children*
(i)   Young people should be free to complete their time at school without unnecessary intrusion.

(ii)   Journalists must not interview or photograph children under the age of 16 on subjects involving the welfare of the child or of any other child, in the absence of or without the consent of a parent or other adult who is responsible for the children.

(iii) Pupils must not be approached or photographed while at school without the permission of the school authorities.

(iv) There must be no payment to minors for material involving the welfare of children nor payment to parents or guardians for material about their children or wards unless it is demonstrably in the child's interest.

(v) Where material about the private life of a child is published, there must be justification for publication other than the fame, notoriety or position of his or her parents or guardian.

7   Children in sex cases*

(i) The press must not, even where the law does not prohibit it, identify children under the age of 16 who are involved in cases concerning sexual offences, whether as victims or as witnesses.

(ii) In any press report of a case involving a sexual offence against a child:

(a) the child must not be identified

(b) the adult may be identified

(c) the word 'incest' must not be used where a child victim might be identified

(d) care must be taken that nothing in the report implies the relationship between the accused and the child.

8   Listening devices*

Journalists must not obtain or publish material obtained by using clandestine listening devices or by intercepting private telephone conversations.

9   Hospitals*

(i) Journalists or photographers making enquiries at hospitals or similar institutions must identify themselves to a responsible executive and obtain permission before entering non-public areas.

(ii) The restrictions on intruding into privacy are particularly relevant to enquiries about individuals in hospitals or similar institutions.

10   Reporting of crime*

(i) The press must avoid identifying relatives or friends of persons convicted or accused of crime without their consent.

(ii) Particular regard should be paid to the potentially vulnerable position of children who are witnesses to, or victims of, crime. This should not be interpreted as restricting the right to report judicial proceedings.

11   Misrepresentation*

(i)   Journalists must not generally obtain or seek to obtain information or pictures through misrepresentation or subterfuge.

(ii)   Documents or photographs should be removed only with the consent of the owner.

(iii) Subterfuge can be justified only in the public interest and only when material cannot be obtained by any other means.

12   Victims of sexual assault
      The press must not identify victims of sexual assault or publish material likely to contribute to such identification unless there is adequate justification and, by law, they are free to do so.

13   Discrimination

(i)   The press must avoid prejudicial or pejorative reference to a person's race, colour, religion, sex or sexual orientation or to any physical or mental illness or disability.

(ii)   It must avoid publishing details of a person's race, colour, religion, sexual orientation, physical or mental illness or disability unless these are directly relevant to the story.

14   Financial journalism

(i)   Even where the law does not prohibit it, journalists must not use for their own profit financial information they receive in advance of its general publication, nor should they pass such information to others.

(ii)   They must not write about shares or securities in whose performance they know that they or their close families have a significant financial interest, without disclosing the interest to the editor or financial editor.

(iii) They must not buy or sell, either directly or through nominees or agents, shares or securities about which they have written recently or about which they intend to write in the near future.

15   Confidential sources
      Journalists have a moral obligation to protect confidential sources of information.

16   Payment for articles*

(i)   Payment or offers of payment for stories or information must not be made directly or through agents to witnesses or potential witnesses in current criminal proceedings except where the material concerned ought to be published in the public interest and there is an overriding need to make or promise to make a payment for this to be done. Journalists must take every possible step to ensure that no financial dealings have influence on the evidence that those witnesses may give. (An editor authorising such a payment must be prepared to demonstrate that there is legitimate public interest at stake involving matters that the public has a right to know. The payment or, where accepted, the offer of payment to any witness who is actually cited to give evidence must be disclosed to the prosecution and the defence and the witness should be advised of this.)

(ii) Payment or offers of payment for stories, pictures or information, must not be made directly or through agents to convicted or confessed criminals or to their associates – who may include family, friends and colleagues – except where the material concerned ought to be published in the public interest and payment is necessary for this to be done.

The public interest

There may be exceptions to the clauses marked * where they can be demonstrated to be in the public interest.

1   The public interest includes:
   (i)   detecting or exposing crime or a serious misdemeanour
   (ii) protecting public health and safety
   (iii) preventing the public from being misled by some statement or action of an individual or organisation.

2   In any case where the public interest is invoked, the Press Complaints Commission will require a full explanation by the editor demonstrating how the public interest was served.

3   There is a public interest in freedom of expression itself. The Commission will therefore have regard to the extent to which material has, or is about to, become available to the public.

4   In cases involving children, editors must demonstrate an exceptional public interest to override the normally paramount interests of the child.

OTHER ISSUES

So much for media law and the professional codes. But what about the issues they don't cover – and your own personal ethical standards? Are there things that some interviewers do that seem to you either morally wrong or at least dubious?

The buy-up interview

For example, what about the buy-up interview, when a publication pays the interviewee for an exclusive? This is often disparaged by the use of the emotive phrase 'chequebook journalism' – some people claim that paying for stories is both lazy and potentially corrupt. They say that journalists should not pay the people they interview because (a) it makes the job too easy and (b) it raises doubts about the authenticity of what is said (as well as being unfair competition for poorer publications).

Before you endorse this view consider two points. First look at the situation from the interviewee's point of view. If they have a story to tell, why shouldn't they sell it? If it's a good story, the publication stands to profit and the interviewer gets a credit as well as being paid. Why shouldn't the interviewee make something out of it?

My view of 'chequebook journalism' changed radically when I was asked by a lawyer to negotiate the sale of an exclusive interview on behalf of a political activist released from jail in a foreign country. The person concerned wanted to be interviewed by a sympathetic journalist. But, having just come out of jail, he also needed money. So – his decision – the story went to the highest bidder, a Sunday tabloid.

Part of the deal, incidentally, was that we had a limited degree of copy approval: the page proofs of the story were to be checked by us to ensure that the interviewee had not accidentally named, and so compromised, other political activists. This, of course, would not have been possible in a free-for-all, such as an open press conference.

(Careful readers will have spotted that this transaction might well have breached clause 16 Payment for articles section (ii) of the PCC code of practice: 'Payment . . . must not be made . . . to convicted or confessed criminals'. Yes indeed, as might the buy-up of an interview with Nelson Mandela, once convicted of terrorism in South Africa and now a revered elder statesman – perhaps this section of the code could be looked at again.)

Second, compare the buy-up interview with the serialisation of a book, particularly a ghosted book (where the 'author' is interviewed by a journalist who effectively writes the book). In ethical terms what's the difference? Yet nobody suggests that the 'author' of a ghosted book shouldn't be paid for 'writing' it or that they shouldn't be paid a second time when it is serialised.

The law of copyright is useful here: it is a reminder that a person normally 'owns' their own words. Thus in a society regulated by money it is surely reasonable that a person should be able to sell an exclusive interview – and therefore, logically, that a publication should be able to buy it.

Freebies

Bribes and 'inducements' (offers of bribes?) are mentioned in the NUJ code, but neither it nor the PCC code refers explicitly to freebies: lunches, trips abroad, cars on loan and other goodies provided to journalists by organisations keen to attract editorial coverage for their products and services. As with 'inducements', the issue is clear-cut: a journalist must not allow them to influence the performance of their professional duties.

Some publications ban their staff from accepting freebies but this is rare: the majority have to learn to live with the fact that Christmas comes more than once a year. And, in general, this is something they're quite good at: the robust, cynical culture of British journalism encourages hacks to sup politely with the devil – then complain in print that the supper was far too hot.

Entertaining

Payment for entertaining rarely poses an ethical problem: when journalists conduct interviews over a drink, who pays for it is usually incidental. But if the interviewee pays, the journalist should obviously not then claim the drinks on expenses.

Privacy

Of all the issues journalists must face, privacy is the most important: it features prominently in the professional codes, and by being included in the European convention on human rights it has become part of the UK legal landscape. And it is the issue that most concerns the politicians, academics, celebrities and other non-journalists who would like to see a more regulated rather than a freer press.

Some politicians are exceptions to the trend: ex-Liberal Democrat leader Paddy Ashdown, for example, told the *Times* when it serialised his diaries in 2000 that he was not in favour of a privacy law. 'I fear it would only serve to protect the rich and powerful,' he said – making the obvious point.

There have been – still are – abuses of people's privacy: reporters on trivial stories doorstepping; bereaved relatives being pursued; hospital patients having unwelcome visitors. But some of the famous/notorious cases of 'press intrusion' aren't quite so straightforward.

The best-known case is that of Princess Diana. In the emotive aftermath of her death in a Paris car crash it was even suggested that its 'cause' was harassment by press photographers. This canard was disposed of by the French inquest which established that Diana's driver was drunk at the time of the crash.

More generally, it is difficult for someone in Diana's position to play the privacy card if they spend so much time trying to manipulate the media. The two most flagrant examples of this were her secret collaboration with Andrew Morton in the writing of *Diana: Her True Story* and the notorious *Panorama* interview in which she announced her intention of becoming the 'Queen of Hearts'.

The same point applies to politicians. Those who electioneer by means of happy-family pix of wife/husband and little ones can hardly complain when the mask is torn away to reveal MP in bed with hooker. Also, if politicians are to be allowed their 'privacy' it will be invoked to cover not just their sexual activities but their financial ones as well.

The other side of the channel provides an awful warning here. French politicians are traditionally allowed their 'privacy' – so the voters usually find out about their various misdemeanours only after their death.

There is a paradox in the current obsession with 'privacy' as an issue. For never before have interviewees – celebrities, royals, politicians, sport stars and ordinary people – been so ready to reveal themselves via the media to the world. The audience demands and enjoys more and more access; their targets are more than ever eager to oblige. Politicians publish their diaries, sports stars their ghosted autobiographies, both full of intimate detail. Celebrities queue up to be paid to appear in magazines like *Hello!* and *OK!*; ordinary people queue up to appear in programmes like *Big Brother*. In this situation blaming the media for abusing people's privacy misses the point. Much of this 'abuse' is really self-abuse.

But the practical issue remains: how far should you go in 'intruding on', 'harassing' and 'pursuing' those you wish to interview? The only possible answer is: it depends on the story. It's not that the end would justify the means if the means were intrinsically evil, but it's reasonable to balance the public good against the private annoyance.

Entrapment

This is the old tabloid trick where the undercover journalist approaches the alleged celebrity drug user/dealer, pretending to sell/use drugs, then writes up the story. In most cases the only justification for the trick is to sell more news-papers. In the honeytrap, sex (or the promise of it) is the bait.

There are signs that while the trick continues to sell papers, it does less damage to the celebrities involved. Rugby star Lawrence Dallaglio, victim of the *News of the World* in 1999, was soon reinstated in the England team; the Earl of Hardwicke, caught by a *News of the World* drugs sting, was later told by the judge 'Were it not for that elaborate sting you would not, I accept, have committed these particular offences' – and escaped a jail sentence.

The ex-tabloid editor Roy Greenslade, who now writes on media issues for the *Guardian*, called the Hardwicke case a landmark moment with the message: 'Drugs may be bad. Drug-dealing may be worse. But journalistic subterfuge is even worse still. By extension therefore tabloid investigators are greater sinners than drug-dealers.'

Attributing quotes

Quotes should be attributed to one named individual. (Avoid suggesting that two or more people used identical words unless they are a music-hall act.) This gives your story authenticity – indeed the stronger and more vivid the quote, the more the reader will want to know who said it.

There are exceptions to this rule. It is general practice not to identify press officers. Their job is to speak on behalf of an organisation so they are its 'spokesman' or 'spokeswoman' (please not, except in parody, 'spokesperson'). But, given the choice, quote a named individual in an organisation rather than its press officer.

This exception has traditionally applied to political briefings, such as those of the parliamentary lobby (specialist reporters covering parliament) by the prime minister's press secretary. But anonymous political briefings are increas-ingly criticised – particularly where they involve character assassination of ministers who have fallen out of favour.

Indeed in both politics and general news it is now argued that pejorative blind quotes are journalistically unethical. Some British journalists now favour the approach of American broadsheet papers such as the *New York Times*, whose stylebook says: 'Anonymity must not become a cloak for attacks on people ...' It is hard to disagree.

In some stories interviewees can't be named because the consequences for them would be devastating: if identified, they would lose their job or their marriage would collapse, and so on. But if you can't name people, try to avoid giving them false names. It is silly to write 'Darren Smith (not his real name)' or 'Darren Smith' with a footnote that says 'The names in this article have been changed'.

Why not simply write 'Darren ——'? Then the reader gets the idea that you're not identifying him and it doesn't matter whether he's actually called Darren or not.

Glossary of terms used in journalism

ABC: Audit Bureau of Circulation – source of circulation figures
advertorial: advertisement presented as editorial
agony aunt: advice giver on personal problems sent in by readers
ambush: journalists lie in wait for unsuspecting interviewee
artwork: illustrations accompanying copy
ascender: portion of lower-case letter that sticks out above the x-height
attribution: identifying source of information or quote

back bench (the): senior newspaper journalists who make key production decisions
backgrounder: explanatory feature to accompany news story
banner (headline): one in large type across front page
bill: poster promoting newspaper, usually highlighting main news story
bleed: (of an image) go beyond the type area to the edge of the page
blob par: extra paragraph introduced by blob/bullet point
blurb: another name for standfirst or similar displayed copy
body copy: the main text of a story as opposed to headings, intro, etc.
body type: the main typeface in which a story is set
bold: thick black type, used for emphasis
breaker: typographical device, such as crosshead, to break up text on the page
broadsheet: large-format newspaper such as *The Times*
bust (to): (of a headline) be too long for the space available
buy-up interview: exclusive interview bought by publication
byline: name of journalist who has written the story

calls: routine phone calls by reporters to organisations such as police and fire brigade
caps: capital letters
cast off (to): estimate length of copy
catchline: single word identifying story typed top right on every page
centre (to): set (headline) with equal space on either side
centre spread: middle opening of tabloid or magazine
chapel: office branch of media union
character: unit of measurement for type including letters, figures, punctuation marks and spaces

chequebook journalism: paying large sums for stories
chief sub: senior journalist in charge of sub-editors
city desk: financial section of British newspaper (US: home news desk)
clippings/clips: press cuttings
colour piece: news story written as feature with emphasis on journalist's reactions
context par: paragraph in feature providing necessary background, often linking intro with what follows
contacts book: a journalist's list of contacts with their phone numbers
copy: text of story
crop (to): cut (image) to size
crosshead: occasional line(s) of type usually bigger and bolder than body type, inserted between paragraphs to liven up page
cut-out: illustration with background masked or cut to make it stand out on the page
cuts: press cuttings

dateline: place from which copy is filed, usually abroad
deadline: time by which a journalist must complete a story
death knock: interview with bereaved person
deck: one of a series of headlines stacked on top of each other
delayed drop: device in news story of delaying important facts for effect
descender: portion of lower-case letter that sticks out below the x-height
deskman: American term for male sub-editor
diary (the): list of news events to be covered; hence an off-diary story is one originated by the reporter
diary column: gossip column
direct input: transmission of copy direct from the journalist's keyboard to the computer for typesetting (as opposed to the old system in which printers retyped copy)
display type: type for headlines, etc.
doorstepping: reporters lying in wait for (usually) celebrities outside their homes
double spread: two facing pages
downtable (subs): those other than the chief sub and deputies
drop cap: initial letter of story or paragraph set in large type alongside first few lines of text (cf. raised cap: large letter raised above text)
dummy: 1 photocopied or printed (but not distributed) version of new publication used for practice and discussion; 2 blank version of established publication, for example, to show weight of paper; 3 complete set of page proofs

edition: version of newspaper printed for particular circulation area or time
editorial: 1 leading article expressing publication's opinion; 2 matter that is not advertising
em, en: units of measurement for type – the width of the two letters m and n
embargo: time before which an organisation supplying material, e.g. by press release, does not want it published
exclusive: claim by newspaper or magazine that it has a story nobody else has

face: type design
feature: article that goes beyond reporting of facts to explain and/or entertain

file (to): transmit copy
fireman: reporter sent to trouble spot when story breaks
flatplan: page-by-page plan of magazine issue
flush left or right: (of type) have one consistent margin with the other ragged
fount: (pronounced 'font' and sometimes spelt that way) typeface
free: free newspaper
freebie: something useful or pleasant, often a trip, supplied free to journalists
freelance: self-employed journalist who sells material to various media
freelancer: American term for freelance
full out: (of type) not indented
full point: full stop

galley proof: typeset proof not yet made up into a page
gutter: space between pages in centre spread

hack/hackette: jocular terms for journalist
hanging indent: set copy with first line of each paragraph full out and subsequent lines indented
heavy: broadsheet newspaper
honeytrap: entrapment of celebrity by sexual seduction
house style: the way a publication chooses to treat matters of detail, e.g. abbreviations

imprint: name and address of publisher and printer
indent: set copy several characters in from left-hand margin
in-house: inside a media organisation
input (to): type copy into computer
insert: extra copy to be included in existing story
intro: first paragraph of story
italics: italic (sloping) type

journo: jocular term for journalist
justified: type set with consistent margins

kill (to): to drop a story; hence 'kill fee' for freelance whose commissioned story is not used
knocking copy: story written with negative angle

layout: arrangement of body type, headlines and illustrations on the page
leader: leading article expressing publication's opinion
leading: (pronounced 'ledding') space between lines (originally made by inserting blank slugs of lead between lines of type)
leg: column of typeset copy
legal (to): check for legal problems such as libel
lensman: American term for male photographer
lift (to): steal a story from another media outlet and reproduce it with few changes
linage: (this spelling preferred to lineage) payment to freelances by the line
listings: lists of entertainment and other events with basic details
literal: typographical error
lobby (the): specialist group of political reporters covering the House of Commons

lower case: ordinary letters (not caps)

make-up: assembly of type and illustrations on the page ready for printing
masthead: newspaper's front-page title
must: copy that must appear, e.g. apology or correction

newsman: American term for male reporter
nib: news in brief – short news item
night lawyer: barrister who reads proofs for legal problems
nub par: paragraph explaining what a feature is essentially about

obit: obituary
off-diary: *see* diary (the)
off-the-record: statements made to a journalist on the understanding that they will
    not be reported directly or attributed
on spec: uncommissioned (material submitted by freelance)
on-the-record: statements made to a journalist that can be reported and attributed
op-ed: feature page facing page with leading articles

page proof: proof of a made-up page
par/para: paragraph
paparazzo/i: photographer(s) specialising in pursuing celebrities
paste-up: page layout pasted into position
pay-off: final twist or flourish in the last paragraph of story
pic/pix: press photograph(s)
pica: unit of type measurement
pick-up: (of photographs) those that already exist, which can therefore be picked
    up by journalists covering a story
piece: article
point: 1 full stop; 2 standard unit of type size
proof: trial impression of typeset matter to be checked
proofread (to): check proofs
puff: copy that praises uncritically and reads like an advertisement
pull-out quotes: short extracts from features set in larger type as part of page
    layout
pyramid: (usually inverted) conventional structure for news story with most
    important facts in intro

query: question mark
quote: verbatim quotation
quotes: quotation marks

range left or right: (of type) have one consistent margin with the other ragged
reverse out: reversal of black and white areas of printed image
roman: plain upright type
RSI: repetitive strain injury attributed to over-use and misuse of computer
    keyboard, mouse, etc.
run on: (of type) continue from one line, column or page to the next
running story: one that is constantly developing, over a newspaper's different
    editions or a number of days
sanserif: a plain typeface (with no serifs)

scoop: jocular word for exclusive
screamer: exclamation mark
sell: another name for standfirst, often used in women's magazines
serif: small, terminating stroke on individual letters/characters, hence serif type
setting: copy set in type
shy: (of headline) too short for the space available
sidebar: self-contained section accompanying main feature
side-head: subsidiary heading
sketch: light-hearted account of events, especially parliamentary
slip: newspaper edition for particular area or event
snap: early summary by news agency of important story to come
snapper: jocular term for press photographer
snaps: press photographs
spike: where rejected copy goes
splash: tabloid's main front-page story
splash sub: sub-editor responsible for tabloid's front page
spoiler: attempt by newspaper to reduce impact of rival's exclusive by publishing similar story
standfirst: introductory matter, particularly used with features
stet: ignore deletion (Latin for 'let it stand')
stone sub: sub-editor who makes final corrections and cuts on page proofs
story: article, especially news report
strap(line): introductory words above main headline
Street (the): Fleet Street, where many newspapers once had their offices
stringer: freelance on contract to a news organisation
sub: sub-editor – journalist who checks, corrects, rewrites copy, writes headlines, captions, etc., and checks proofs; on newspapers, but not on most magazines, subs are also responsible for layout

tabloid: popular small-format newspaper such as the *Sun*
taster: production journalist who checks and selects copy
think piece: feature written to show and provoke thought
tip: information supplied, and usually paid for, whether by freelance or member of the public
totty: triumph over tragedy, feature formula particularly popular in women's magazines
typo: American term for typographical error

underscore: underline
upper case: capital letters

vox pop: series of street interviews (Latin: *vox populi* – voice of the people)

widow: line of type consisting of a single word or syllable
wob: white on black – type reversed out

x-height: height of the lower-case letters of a typeface (excluding ascenders and descenders)

Further reading

General

Graham Greene's novel *Stamboul Train* includes a portrait of an investigative reporter, Mabel Warren. The German political activist Gunter Wallraff worked undercover for extended periods both using and subverting journalistic techniques. The Robert Harris trilogy is investigative journalism at its best.

Day, Robin, *Grand Inquisitor*, Weidenfeld & Nicholson, 1989.
Greene, Graham, *Stamboul Train*, Penguin, 1992.
Harris, Robert, *The Media Trilogy: Gotcha!, Selling Hitler, Good and Faithful Servant*, Faber & Faber, 1994.
Knightley, Phillip, *A Hack's Progress*, Viking, 1997.
Mitford, Jessica, *The Making of a Muckraker*, Quartet, 1980, out of print.
Simpson, John, *Strange Places, Questionable People*, Macmillan, 1998.
Wallraff, Gunter, *The Lowest of the Low*, Methuen, 1985.
—— *Wallraff the Undesirable Journalist*, Pluto Press, 1978.
Wolfe, Tom, and Johnson E. W. (eds), *The New Journalism*, Picador, 1990.

Interview collections

Lynn Barber's two books include excellent introductions.

Barber, Lynn, *Mostly Men*, Viking, 1991.
—— *Demon Barber*, Viking, 1998.
Broughton, F. (ed.) *Time Out Interviews 1968–1998*, Penguin, 1998.
Davies, Hunter, *Hunting People: Thirty Years of Interviews with the Famous*, Mainstream Publishing, 1994.
Silvester, Christopher (ed.), *The Penguin Book of Interviews*, Viking, 1993.
Terkel, Studs, *Working*, Penguin, 1985.

Insight into politics

Anonymous, *Primary Colors*, Vintage, 1996.
Dobbs, Michael, *House of Cards*, Collins, 1989.
Jones, N. *Soundbites and Spin Doctors: How Politicians Manipulate the Media – and Vice Versa*, Cassell, 1995.

Stephanopoulos, George, *All Too Human*, Hutchinson, 1999.

Techniques

Berne, Eric, *What Do You Say After You Say Hello?*, Andre Deutsch, 1974.
McCrum, Sarah, and Hughes, Lotte, *Interviewing Children*, Save The Children, 1998.
    Obtainable from STC, 17 Grove Lane, London SE5 8RD (tel. 020 7703 5400).
Markham, Ursula, *How to Deal with Difficult People*, Thorsons, 1993.

Law and ethics

Belsey, A., and Chadwick, R., *Ethical Issues in Journalism*, Routledge, 1992.
Bonnington, A. J., McKain, B. and Watt, G. A., *Scots Law for Journalists*, W. Green
    & Son, 1995.
Carter-Ruck, Peter, *Carter-Ruck on Libel and Slander*, Butterworths, 1997.
Greenwood, Walter and Welsh, Tom, *McNae's Essential Law for Journalists*,
    Butterworths, 1999.
Kieran, Matthew, (ed.), *Media Ethics*, Routledge, 1998.
Malcolm, Janet, *The Journalist and the Murderer*, Bloomsbury, 1991.
Mason, Peter, and Smith, Derek, *Magazine Law: A Practical Guide*,
    Routledge/Blueprint 1998.
Robertson, Geoffrey, and Nicol, Andrew, *Media Law*, Penguin, 1992.
Snoddy, Raymond, *The Good, the Bad and the Unacceptable: The Hard News about the
    British Press*, Faber & Faber, 1993.
Wilson, John, *Understanding Journalism: A Guide to Issues*, Routledge, 1996.

Appendix 1
Miles Kington on celebrity interviews

Q. What is an interview?
A. An interview is an encounter between an unknown person and a famous person, for which the unknown person gets paid but the celebrity does not.

Q. Why should a celebrity undergo this ordeal?
A. To keep in touch with the public while only having to meet one of them. To put straight mistakes made by the previous interviewer. To publicise a book or film. Because he has been told to.

Q. What does the interviewer get out of it?
A. An autograph for his children.

Q. What does it mean when an interviewer says: 'He paused and thought deeply before replying'?
A. It means the celebrity is trying to remember the answer he always gives to this question.

Q. Does he always give the same answers?
A. Yes.

Q. Why?
A. Because he is always asked the same questions.

Q. How does an interviewer prepare for an interview?
A. He looks up cuttings of previous interviews with the celebrity to see what kind of questions have been asked before.

Q. And then?
A. He asks them again.

Q. What if the interviewer actually does ask different, new questions?
A. The celebrity pauses and thinks deeply, then gives the same old answers.

Q. What is the question most often asked in interviews?
A. 'What sort of difference has fame made to your private life?'

Q. What is the answer to that question?
A. 'It means I have to suffer interviews by odious little nerks like you.'

Q. Does he actually say that?
A. No. He says: 'I have very little private life, but I owe everything to the public, and never resent their intrusion.'

Q. Does the celebrity manage to correct mistakes made by previous interviewers?
A. Yes.

Q. Does this make him happy?
A. No. A new interviewer always makes new mistakes.

Q. What is the difference between a good interviewer and a bad interviewer?
A. A bad interviewer, when writing his piece, always mentions where it took place. 'As we took tea together in the Ritz', or 'Sitting in his elegant work-room, hung with Hockneys' . . .

Q. Are there any other kinds of interview?
A. Yes, the *Radio Times* interview. This always takes place during the actual production of the star's programme, as if to create the impression that the interviewer is talking to him during the white-hot moment of creation.

Q. And is this the impression created?
A. No. We get the impression that the star is too busy to see the interviewer.

Q. How does the interviewer describe the celebrity?
A. As smaller than I had expected.

Q. What do celebrities most like talking about?
A. Their new books or films. But they find this difficult.

Q. Why?
A. Because interviewers prefer talking about their old books and films.

Q. How long does an interview take?
A. About an hour less than the interview contrives to suggest.

Q. Why do so many interviewers end with 'And there, regretfully, I had to leave it.'
A. Because he is being kicked out.

Q. Why?
A. Because someone else is waiting to interview the celebrity. And there, regretfully, we shall have to leave it.

(Miles Kington, *The Independent*, 12 June 1987. Used with permission of *The Independent*)

Appendix 2
Madonna interviewed as never before

'Are you a bold hussy-woman that feasts on men who are tops?' – 'Yes, yes, this brings to the surface my longings'

In 1996, Madonna spoke to Hungarian magazine *Blikk*. The questions were asked in Hungarian and translated into English. Madonna's replies were then translated into Hungarian. The interview was published in Hungarian and finally translated back into English. When *Time* Magazine reproduced this journalistic gem, it commented: 'To say that something was lost in the process is to be wildly ungrateful for all that was gained.' (These extracts, incidentally, are plucked from cyberspace.)

Blikk: Madonna, Budapest says hello with arms that are spreadeagled. Did you have a visit here that was agreeable? Are you in good odour? You are the biggest fan of our young people who hear your musical productions and like to move their bodies in response.

Madonna: Thank you for saying these compliments [holds up hands]. Please stop with taking sensationalist photographs until I have removed my garments for all to see [laughs]. This is a joke I have made.

Blikk: Madonna, let's cut toward the hunt. Are you a bold hussy-woman that feasts on men who are tops?

Madonna: Yes, yes, this is certainly something that brings to the surface my longings. In America it is not considered to be mentally ill when a woman advances on her prey in a discotheque setting with hardy cocktails present. And there is a more normal attitude toward leather play-tops that also makes my day.

Blikk: Tell us this how you met Carlos, your love servant who is reputed? Did you know he was heaven-sent right off the stick? Or were you dating many other people in your bed at the same time?

Madonna: No, he was the only one I was dating in my bed then, so it is a scientific fact that the baby was made in my womb using him. But as regards those questions, enough! I am a woman and not a test-mouse! Carlos is an everyday person who is in the orbit of a star who is being muscle-trained by him, not a sex machine.

Blikk: May we talk about your other 'baby' your movie, then? Please do not be denying that the similarities between you and the real Evita are grounded in basis. Power, money, tasty-food, Grammys – all these elements are afoot.

Madonna: What is up in the air with you? Evita never was winning a Grammy!

Blikk: Perhaps not. But as to your film, in trying to bring your reputation along a rocky road, can you make people forget the bad explosions of *Who's That Girl?* and *Shanghai Surprise?*

Madonna: I am a tip-top starlet. That is the job that I am paid to do.

Blikk: OK, here's a question from left space. What was your book *Slut* about?

Madonna: It was called *Sex*, my book.

Blikk: Not in Hungary. Here it was called *Slut*. How did it come to publish? Were you lovemaking with an about-town printer? Do you prefer making suggestive literature to fast-selling CDs?

Madonna: These are different facets to my career highway. I am preferring only to become respected all over the map as a 100 per cent artist.

Blikk: There is much interest in you from this geographical region, so I must ask this final questions. How many Hungarian men have you dated in bed? Are they No 1? How are they comparing to Argentine men, who are famous for being tip-top as well?

Madonna: Well, to avoid aggravating global tension, I won't say. It's a tie [laughs]. No, no, I am serious now. See here I am working like a canine all the way around the clock! I am too busy even to try the goulash that makes your country for the record books.

Blikk: Thank you for your candid chitchat.

Madonna: No problem, friend who is a girl.

(*Source: Evening Standard*, 14 August 1998)

Appendix 3
Bob Woodward interview request

Bob Woodward, assistant managing editor of the Washington *Post*, writes to President Bill Clinton requesting an interview.

This extract from Woodward's masterly letter is taken from *All Too Human* (1999), George Stephanopoulos's account of his time working as campaign manager, later press secretary to Bill Clinton. The comments are from Stephanopoulos.

> Woodward knew his subject and his potential source. He opened with a bland understatement:
>
> > I believe you are aware that I am writing a book on government economic policy-making. The book already has a heavy and growing emphasis on your administration.
>
> Followed by intimidation:
>
> > I already have accumulated more than 100 pages of typed notes, memos, recollections, charts, and tables on just one of the pre-Inaugural meetings you had with your economic team . . .
>
> Obligatory humility:
>
> > But I have wondered many times, what am I missing? A lot, no doubt – too much. My reporting has yielded enough that I am definitely humbled by what I don't know . . . Though much of what I have comes from the inside, I've written enough about government and Presidents to know that the most powerful inside account is still really from the outside. It lacks the perspective of the President . . .
>
> An appeal to history:
>
> > Richard Reeves, in his remarkable new book on President Kennedy, *Profile of Power*, poses the graphic and compelling question: What is it really like to be President? . . . Reeves was forced to rely on substantial documentary records and the testimony of others near, but not at, the very center. He never interviewed Kennedy . . .
>
> A civic-minded slap at the press:

Just in eight months, it's clear that you've been on a singular journey. But the published and broadcast accounts of it miss far too much. Public dialogue is at too low a level. Aren't the problems of governing connected to the shallow discourse? . . .

Fair warning and reassurance:

Might it involve some loss of control and some risk? Yes . . . [But] I don't intend a how's-he-doing assessment . . . No cheap shots. No cheerleading . . .

And a big, flattering, irresistible finish:

In my last book, *The Commanders* . . . I ended the introduction with this idea: 'The decision to go to war is one that defines a nation, both to the world and, perhaps more importantly, to itself. There is no more serious business for a national government, no more accurate measure of national leadership.'

I wrote that in the spring of 1991. About that time, you made the point to friends and associates that the battlefield had shifted. National self-definition, seriousness and leadership would next be measured by economic and domestic policy. You were right.

It worked. Clinton agreed to meet Woodward.

Appendix 4
On the receiving end

Stephanopoulos in the same book *All Too Human* describes his interview with Woodward over a meal at Woodward's home.

> His dining-room table was topped with neatly stacked, typed notes and a pocket tape recorder ... He hit me with memos from one of our first economic meetings, then some hand-written notes from another, followed by word-for-word transcripts of what I had said at a third. Woodward's technique is no less effective for being so obvious. He flashes a glimpse of what he knows, shaded in a largely negative light, with a hint of more to come, setting up a series of prisoner's dilemmas in which each prospective source faces a choice: Do you cooperate and elaborate in return (you hope) for learning more and earning a better portrayal – for your boss and yourself? Or do you call his bluff by walking away in the hope that your reticence will make the final product less authoritative and therefore less damaging? If no one talks, there is no book. But someone – then everyone – always talks. The deadliest initial response was my instinctive one: 'Well, it wasn't like that exactly ...' 'Really? *Innnn*teresting ... I didn't *know* that ... Tell me ...'
>
> Our dance had begun, the mutual seduction of reporter and source. Woodward's calculated charm was custom tailored to my intellectual vanity, professional pride and personal loyalty to the president.

The word to applaud and learn from here is 'mutual seduction'. Stephanopoulos has the honesty to admit that being a 'source' to a famous investigative reporter is really an act of self-aggrandisement.

Index